THIS SIDE OF

WILD

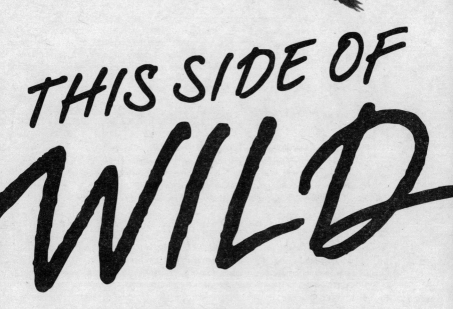

THIS SIDE OF WILD

MUTTS, MARES, and LAUGHING DINOSAURS

GARY PAULSEN

Illustrated by Tim Jessell

SCHOLASTIC INC.

ISBN 978-1-338-13159-8

Text copyright © 2015 by Gary Paulsen. Illustrations copyright © 2015 by Tim Jessell. All rights reserved.
Published by Scholastic Inc., 557 Broadway, New York, NY 10012, by arrangement with
Simon & Schuster Books for Young Readers, an imprint of Simon & Schuster Children's Publishing Division.
SCHOLASTIC and associated logos are trademarks and/or registered trademarks of Scholastic Inc.

12 11 10 9 8 7 6 5 4   17 18 19 20 21

Printed in the U.S.A.   40

First Scholastic printing, November 2016

Book design by Krista Vossen
The text for this book is set in Fournier.
The illustrations for this book are rendered in pen and ink.

To Mike Kelly—who knows
—G. P.

To those who can hear the primal call of the wild
and the inspiration and humble majesty it bares
—T. J.

CONTENTS

INTRODUCTION: ALONE

I crossed the Pacific Ocean the first time when I was seven years old, in 1946. We, my mother and I, were headed to meet my father in the Philippine Islands, where we would live for three years. Because flying was still very risky and extremely expensive, we took a troop ship filled with soldiers and sailors, which fairly crawled across the water.

The Pacific was—and is, of course—huge; it's the largest single entity on the planet. All the land masses of all the other parts of the earth would easily fit in it with water left over. The ship, as the cliché says, was very small, and *on* the ship, I was correspondingly even more tiny, so that one would think I would feel dwarfed, alienated in some way.

In fact, just the opposite happened: I loved it. The incredible blue that stretched up and away to the horizon drew me in, embraced me, made me feel that I was a part of it, and I remember sitting day after day (my mother was almost clinically seasick) in the bow of the rusted old Victory ship (it had just gone through the entire Second World War and had survived—barely), marveling that such a thing would be, *could* be. In the distance now and then I would see dolphins; closer in, flying fish; and still closer, at the stern, sharks waiting for the daily garbage from the galley. But they did not seem to be part of my relationship with the ocean; they seemed separate in some way.

The ocean was what drew me then, and I knew it would pull me in all my life. Later, when I discovered sailing, it was completely natural that I would sail on the Pacific by myself. It was like coming home.

And it was here, three hundred miles off the coast of California in a twenty-two-foot Schock-designed sloop, sailing single-handed, that I would come to know—to *know*—how small a part of everything I really happened to be.

It was night, cloudless but with a marine layer of haze that dampened even any light from the stars. Pitch-dark, inside-of-a-dead-cow black-night dark, and as it so often seemed to happen, the wind completely stopped. Not only was the wind dead around me but dead for hundreds of miles to the north as well, for there were no swells, no motion whatsoever in the water coming down from the north. The boat drifted in aimless, small circles, as still as if we were on a tiny pond in somebody's yard. I had never seen it so still and quiet, and I poured a cup of hot tea from my thermos and sat sipping it, thinking in all the world—in all the planets in all the worlds—I was alone, completely and vastly and wonderfully alone.

Alone.

And precisely at that moment a young gray whale,

completely unsuspected, unheard, came up alongside and lay his or her head across the stern of the boat, virtually in my lap, pushing the boat down so hard it seemed about to roll over. Then, blowing a huge spout of snotty air, it slid backward off the boat and back under the water and was gone.

I remember precisely what happened next.

I stopped breathing.

And I spilled my tea.

And I realized we are never quite alone.

PREFACE: THE LEARNING PROCESS

Finally, after many attempts and filled-out forms for the military bureaucracy, I had been given permission to ride on a horse and explore that portion of the great southern desert known as Mcregor Missile and Bombing Range, which is located north and slightly east of El Paso, Texas. It has been in use almost constantly since the Second World War, or nearly, and is pocketed with craters from explosions and spotted here and there with blue painted target bombs that were not meant to explode but simply made a puff when they landed.

More important for my uses, the area had once, in pre-history, been along a water course that flowed past a series of tall buttes, fed in an unmeasured ancient prehistory by mountain streams and snowmelt that has long since dried up. In that long-ago time, the people who lived along this course worked at making pottery, and there was wonderful beauty in it. The people, however, had not learned to make pottery-curing ovens to bake it. Instead they would pile the freshly formed and painted pots interlaced with sun-dried mesquite and make a bonfire of the whole pile.

Some of the pots would make it and would be fired and ring true to a testing finger snap and be useful for gathering food and carrying water. Others, perhaps most of the clay pots, from the way it appeared, cracked and broke into shards in the crude heat and were left in clumps in the desert. The ash blew and washed away, leaving the shards to cure in the heat and sun for the hundreds, perhaps thousands, of years down to the present.

Many of the shards were of significant size—two, three inches across—large enough so that the patterns and beauty of the design could still be easily seen and appreciated. Always in brown or black or gray earth pigments, the patterns themselves would be lightning bolts, or snake lines, or rippling water signs, or dancing clouds, or line drawings of deer or small animals or lizards. . . .

They were . . . all . . . incredibly beautiful. The law forbade taking any of the shards, which seemed particularly absurd, considering they were smack in the middle of a bomb and missile range, bound to be hit and destroyed eventually. But that, the likelihood of their temporary nature, perhaps made them even more powerful in their beauty.

I sketched and memorized some of them and rode endless miles over many days from shard pile to shard pile and came to realize that there were many similarities among them, as if people in one area were trying to mimic or communicate with people from another—should they see one another's pots. And farther north, sixty or seventy miles, there was a place called Three Rivers, where there were thousands of petroglyphs on a shallow ridge, and many of *those* drawings seemed very like the drawings on the shards.

Maps, I thought, to water or good soil or good hunting? Messages of joy or happiness or love? Or portraits of lives?

At first I became enthralled and then, finally, obsessed. I found pile after pile of shards, worked intently from one to the next, and was so caught up in it that soon the mare I was riding caught it from me, started looking for signs of the little piles of clay shards as day after day we made search patterns back and forth across the desert. I slept in the horse trailer with her alongside in a wire corral at night, fed her hay from the back of my old truck and water from plastic jerricans, and each day we set off in a new direction: out five to seven miles, over half a mile, then back, pile to pile, trying to learn more about these ancient people, what the art said, meant. . . .

Until.

I carried ration water for traveling in a plastic tube in back of my saddle cantle and watered her in my hat. It was a hot, muggy day, and I realized suddenly that the mare had been sweating excessively and needed water. At the same moment, she and I spotted a new pile of shards along a small gully some ten feet ahead, and I felt her interest quicken as I pulled her over and swung off to the ground, thinking to water her first before looking at the pottery, my eyes on the shards that lay in a generally larger pile than some of the others.

I undid the water tube, took one, two steps toward her front end, and felt the click/slam/push of a rattlesnake hitting my ankle. It hit me in silence, then rattled. . . .

And changed my whole life.

I do not have an inordinate fear of snakes, not even rattlers. In fact, I kind of like them. They have their own living to make—and it is a hard one, living two inches off the ground, no legs, every animal an enemy—and I have mine. I have seen many of them, along with other venomous snakes, and we have always gotten along.

More, still more, I dress sensibly in snake country, wearing high boots, not reaching under rocks without looking closely first. And as a point of fact, on this day, I had heavy cowboy riding boots on, which adequately covered any area a snake would hit.

But there it was. He struck. He *hit* me, tried to do bodily harm to me, and logic, sense, all thinking went right out the door, and I reacted automatically, in sheer, stark terror.

I leaped.

I did not jump, or hop, or run—I leaped like a gazelle. I swear I was four feet off the ground, curving in slow motion, with a kind of death-welcoming grace, and I looked down as I moved up, expecting to see him going away.

No.

Instead he was coming with me! I was wearing good boots, as I said, and heavy jeans over that, and he had penetrated the jeans with his fangs, and both fangs had curved over when he hit the hard leather of the boot, curved back and tangled in the jeans.

I went crazy.

Understand, I had not been bitten. He did not get through the boot. Everything was fine.

But I went absolutely, stark raving mad. I had jumped away, I thought, and yet he was still there.

I shook.

First my ankle, then my leg, then my whole body, whipping the snake back and forth, up and down, around and around as I rose—like a great, spastic animal, shaking until when I came down, slammed down, I looked and he was gone.

I reached back to the saddle horn—the mare had stood still through all of this—and hung there, like a rag doll, and thought how grateful I was that he had not somehow bitten above the boot when I was flying around. Thought how I hoped he had a good home and would have a good and long life and how I hoped and prayed I would never see him again attached to my left ankle; I did not right then think—but would later—of the two very important lessons he had taught me in those few seconds.

First, always, always try to have what the army calls "situational awareness." That is, try to know all that is around you. And second, always, always watch where you put your feet.

THIS SIDE OF
WILD

· CHAPTER ONE ·

A Confusion of Horses, a Border Collie named Josh, a Grizzly Bear Who Liked Holes, and a Poodle with Three Teeth

⊱─────◆─────⊰

First, a hugely diversionary trail:

Very few paths are completely direct, and this one seemed at first to be almost insanely devious.

The doctor diagnosed various problems, some lethal, all apparently debilitating, and left me taking various medications and endless rituals of check-ins and checkouts and tests and retests. . . .

Which drove me almost directly away from the whole process. I moved first to Wyoming, a small town called Story, near Sheridan, where I kept staring at the beauty of the Bighorn Mountains, accessed by a trail out of Story, and at last succumbed to the idea of two horses, one for riding and one for packing.

The reasoning was this: I simply could not stand what I had become—stale, perhaps, or stalemated by what appeared to be my faltering body. Clearly I could not hike the Bighorns, or at least I thought I could not (hiking, in any case, was something I had come to dislike—hate—courtesy of the army), and so to horses.

My experience with riding horses was most decidedly limited. As a child on farms in northern Minnesota, I had worked with workhorse teams—mowing and raking hay, cleaning barns with crude sleds and manure forks—and in the summer we would sometimes ride these workhorses.

They were great, massive (weighing more than a ton), gentle animals and so huge that to get on their backs we either had to climb their legs—like shinnying up a living, hair-covered tree—or get them to stand near a board fence or the side of a hayrack (a wagon with tall wheels and a flatbed used for hauling hay from the field to the barn) so we could jump up and over onto their backs.

Once we were on their backs, with a frantic kicking of bare heels and amateur screaming of what we thought were correct-sounding obscenities—mimicked from our elders—and goading, they could sometimes be persuaded to plod slowly across the pasture while we sat and pretended to be Gene Autry or Roy Rogers—childhood cowboy heroes who never shot to kill but always neatly shot the guns from the bad guys' hands and never kissed the damsels but rode off into the sunset at the end of the story. We would ride down villains who robbed stagecoaches or in other ways threatened damsels in distress, whom we could save and, of course, never kiss, but ride off at the end of our imagination.

The horses were—always—gentle and well behaved, and while they looked nothing like Champion or Trigger—Gene's and Roy's wonderful, pampered, combed, and shampooed lightning steeds (Champ was a bay, a golden brown, as I remember it, and Trigger was a palomino, with a blond, flowing mane and tail)—we

were transformed into cowboys. With our crude, wood-carved six-guns and battered straw garden hats held on with pieces of twine, imagined with defined clarity that the pasture easily became the far Western range and every bush hid a marauding stage robber or a crafty rustler bent on stealing the poor rancher (my uncle, the farmer) blind.

Oh, it was not always so smooth. While they were wonderfully gentle and easy-minded, they had rules, and when those rules were broken, sometimes their retaliation was complete and devastating. On Saturday nights we went to the nearby town—a series of wood-framed small buildings, all without running water or electricity—wherein lived seventy or eighty people. There was a church there and a saloon, and in back of the saloon an added-on frame shack building with a tattered movie screen and a battery-operated small film projector. They showed the same Gene Autry film all the time, and in this film, Gene jumped out of the second story of a building onto the back of a waiting horse.

We, of course, had to try it, and I held the horse—or tried to—while my friend jumped from the hayloft opening in the barn onto the horse's waiting back.

He bounced once—his groin virtually destroyed—made a sound like a broken water pump, slid down the horse's leg, and was kicked in a flat trajectory straight to the rear through the slatted-board wall of the barn. He lived, though I still don't quite know how; his flying body literally knocked the boards from the wall.

I personally went the way of the Native Americans and made a bow of dried willow, with arrows of river cane sharpened to needlepoints and fletched crudely with tied-on chicken feathers plucked from the much-offended egg layers in the coop, which I used to hunt "buffalo" off the back of Old Jim.

Just exactly where it went wrong we weren't sure, but I'm fairly certain that nobody had ever shot an arrow from Old Jim's back before. And I'm absolutely positive that no one had shot said arrow so that the feathers brushed his ears on the way past.

The "buffalo" was a hummock of black dirt directly in front of Jim, and while I couldn't get him into a run, or even a trot, no matter what I tried, I'm sure he was moving at a relatively fast walk when I drew my mighty willow bow and sent the cane shaft at the pile of dirt.

Just for the record, and no matter what my relatives might say, I did *not* hit the horse in the back of his head.

Instead the arrow went directly between Jim's ears, so low the chicken feathers brushed the top of his head as they whistled past.

The effect was immediate and catastrophic. Old Jim somehow gave a mighty one-ton shrug so that all his enormous strength seemed to be focused on squirting me straight into the air like a pumpkin seed, and I fell, somer-saulting in a shower of cane arrows and the bow, with a shat-tering scream on my part and hysterical laughter on the part of the boy with me.

"You looked like a flying porcupine!" he yelled. "Stickers going everywhere . . . You was lucky you wasn't umpaled."

Which was largely true and seemed to establish the modus operandi for the rest of my horse-riding life. I do know that I couldn't get close to Old Jim if I had anything that even remotely resembled a stick for the rest of that summer.

Horses are unique in many ways, though—and I know there will be wild disagreement here—not as smart as dogs, certainly when it comes to math.

I knew nothing of them then and perhaps little more now. But one of those summers I experimented with rodeo.

I was not good at it, to say the very least, and for me it was a particularly stupid thing to do because I was indeed so incredibly bad at it, and I did not do it for any length of time.

I tried bareback bronc riding for a few weeks. I learned some things: I learned intimately how the dirt in Montana tasted and learned that next to old combat veteran infantry sergeants, rodeo riders are the toughest (and kindest and most helpful) people on earth.

But I learned absolutely nothing about horses. I rarely made a good ride, a full ride, but even if I had, you cannot learn much in eight seconds on an animal's back. . . .

And so to the Bighorn Mountains.

It is probably true that all mountains are beautiful; there is something about them, the quality of bigness, of an ethereal joy to their size and scenic quality. And I have seen mountain ranges in Canada, the United States, particularly Alaska, have run sled dogs in them and through them and over them and have been immersed in their beauty as with the old Navajo prayer:

Beauty behind me
Beauty before me
Beauty to my left
Beauty to my right
All around me is beauty.

But there is something special about the Bighorns in Wyoming.

I found a small house at the base of a dirt track called the Penrose Trail, which led directly up out of the town of Story into the lower peaks and a huge hay meadow called Penrose Park.

If memory serves, it is twenty or so miles from Story

up to the meadow, then a few more miles to an old cabin on a lake and the beginning of a wilderness trail through staggering beauty; the trail is called the Solitude Trail—among other nicknames—and it wanders through some seventy miles of mountains in a large loop.

Older people who lived in Story, who rode the mountains before there were trails, told me of the beauty in the high country, and it became at first a lure, a pull, and then almost a drive.

I wanted to see the country, the high country, as I had seen it in Alaska with dog teams; the problem here was that it was summer, too hot for dogs, the distances were much too great, and my dislike of hiking much too sincere for me to even consider backpacking through the mountains.

And so, to horse.

Unfortunately, I knew little or nothing as to how one goes about acquiring a horse to ride on potentially dangerous mountain trails.

And then another horse to pack gear on those same possibly dangerous mountain trails.

For those who have read of my trials and tribulations when I tried to learn how to run dogs for the Iditarod, you will note a great many similarities in the learning procedure, or more accurately, how the learning processes for both endeavors strongly resembled a train wreck. It is true that I have for most of my life lived beneath the military concept that "there is absolutely no substitute for personal inspection at zero altitude" when it comes to trying to learn something. While functional, the problem with this theory is that it often places you personally and physically at the very nexus of destruction. Hence both legs broken, both arms broken more than once, wrists broken, teeth knocked out, ribs cracked and broken, both thumbs broken more than once (strangely more painful than the other breaks) and—seemingly impossible—an arrow self-driven through my left thumb.

Among other bits of lesser mayhem . . .

I had read many Westerns, of course, doing research, and had even written several, had indeed won the Spur Award from the Western Writers of America three times for Western novels. This is perhaps indicative of excess glibness, considering how little I apparently knew. But I had read all those books and seen God knows how many Western films and knew that people had used packhorses. I had run two Iditarod sled-dog races across Alaska, and I thought—really, it seemed to be that simple—that if a person could do one, he could do the other.

The problem was that I did not know anyone involved with horses and so—as God is my witness—I went to the yellow pages for Sheridan, Wyoming (the nearest town of any size), looked under "horse," and near the end of the section, found a listing of horse brokers. (This was before there was a viable Internet to use.)

Perfect, I thought. There were people who bought and sold horses—exactly what I needed. The first two names I called were not available, but on the third call, a gruff voice answered with a word that sounded like "haaawdy" and then asked, "Whut due ya'll need . . . ?"

"It's simple, really," I answered. "I need two horses. One to ride, one to carry a pack. I want to go up into the Bighorn Mountains. . . ."

"Why, sure you do." There was a pause, a long pause. I would surmise later, when I knew more of horse brokers, that he either thought I was joking, or, if he were very lucky, that I was uncompromisingly green, bordering on being perhaps medically stupid, and he had a chance to make his profit for the year on a one- or two-horse deal.

It was, of course, closer to the latter.

"Where do you live?" he asked.

"Story." I named the small town at the base of the Bighorns, near where the Penrose Trail comes out, or down and out. I had purchased a small house there with a few acres of thick grass, and I was surprised to find it vacant. I was to find later—and there were so many "laters" when dealing with Wyoming—near the end of October, why this was to be, when the first late-October snow, a crushing thirty-two inches, came in one day, followed two days later by another thirty inches.

But back then I was wonderfully innocent; it was a grand summer day and the mountains beckoned, pulled, demanded that I come to them as I had in winter in Alaska with dogs during the Iditarod. "Where should I come?" I asked.

"No," he said quickly. "I'll come to you with the horses. I have two that are perfect for you."

"Well, let me . . ." I was going to say, "Let me get ready for them," as I had no idea what one did, really, to have and keep horses. The property had a small pasture with two feet of grass and a three-sided shed, was surrounded by tall ponderosa pines for shade and little else.

But he hung up before I could get another word out, and it seemed that I had just turned around when a large, gaudy pickup hooked to a flashy two-horse trailer pulled into the driveway. It's difficult to describe it without lapsing into poor taste; indeed, the truck and trailer alone were a monument to the word "god-awful." The color was an eye-ripping red with black rubber mudguards, and on each mudguard was a chrome silhouette of a nude woman, and across the front of the hood was—I swear—an actual six-foot-wide longhorn mounted in a silver boss with an engraving (again, I couldn't make this up) of another nude woman with impossibly large features, which was, in turn, matched by the mudguards on the trailer and a large painted silhouette of a nude on the front of the trailer cleverly positioned so that a small ventilation opening for the horses to put their heads out . . . Well, you get the picture.

And if the truck and trailer were in bad taste, they were nothing compared to the man. Tall but with a large beer belly covered by an enormous silver and gold belt buckle with RODEO engraved over yet another silhouette of a nude woman, on top of tailor-cut jeans tucked inside knee-high white cowboys boots with (a major change in art forms) a bright blue bald eagle stitched on the front.

On his head was an impossibly large cowboy hat with a silver hatband, which I at first thought was made of little conchos but turned out to be little silhouettes of, right . . . more women.

He shook my hand without speaking, turned and opened the back of the trailer, and let two horses step out at the same time, which meant they weren't tied in, nor did they have butt chains on—two major mistakes that prove he knew little about trailering horses and hence little about horses themselves.

Not that it mattered. I had already made up my mind that looking in the yellow pages cold for a horse broker was Very Wrong and that I wouldn't buy a horse from this guy if he gave them away.

And yet . . .

And yet . . .

A thing happened, something I had never seen before.

The horses were simply standing there, at relative peace—no nervousness at all—and there was something about them that seemed, well, inviting. And I thought, felt, that I should go to them and touch them, pet them. I know how that sounds, and I have never been all "woo-woo" about animals, especially horses, of which I knew little except that they were big, huge, nine hundred to a thousand pounds, and potentially dangerous. Very dangerous. Decidedly so if they were startled or panicked or surprised. At that time I had had two friends killed while riding them and knew of several others permanently in wheelchairs. (This was years before actor Christopher Reeve, who as an excellent, Olympic-level rider, was permanently completely disabled—which led directly to his later death—when falling on a simple training jump.)

I actually took a step toward them—worse, toward their rear ends, which is *never* the way you walk up on a strange horse—before stopping.

Josh, my border collie, my friend, had been at my side watching, and before I could move farther, he rose from a sitting position, trotted forward, and without hesitating at all, trotted between the back legs of the mare, paused beneath her belly, then continued up through the front legs.

At that moment she lowered her head and they touched noses, whereupon Josh turned to the right, touched noses with the black horse, who had lowered his head, trotted between his front legs, paused under the belly, through his back legs, then back in front of me, where he sat, looked up and—I swear—nodded.

Or it seemed that he nodded.

Or he wanted to nod.

Or he wanted me to *think* that he nodded.

Or he wanted me to know something. Something good about the horses.

What we had witnessed—the broker and I—had been nothing less than a kind of miracle. Dogs, perhaps many dogs, had been killed simply by getting too close to the back feet of a horse. Years later I would acquire a horse who had mistakenly killed his owner, a young woman who was checking his back feet, when a dog came too close. As it kicked at the dog, the horse caught the woman in the chest with a glancing blow. The force was so powerful it severed her aorta and she bled to death before help could arrive.

For Josh to so nonchalantly trot through the mare's legs, as well as the legs of the black cow pony, then back to me, came in the form of a message. . . .

And I listened.

I had by that time lived with dogs, run with dogs, camped with dogs, for literally thousands and thousands of joyous and not a little educational miles. I had been saved, my life saved, many times by dogs—mainly lead dogs—making decisions about bad ice or moose attacks in the night, and I had learned again and again of my own frailty, slowness of thought and action compared to what the dogs could accomplish. And while at first I had trouble believing, because I was as chauvinistic as most humans are, at last I surrendered my own will and abilities to that of the dogs, and when Josh gave his okay to the horses, I listened and bought the horses no matter my feelings for the broker. And the four of us—horses, dog, and I—spent a wonderful summer exploring the wilderness areas of the Bighorn Mountains in Wyoming.

And through all of it—swimming rivers, climbing impossible ridges and grades, running into bear, moose, and one unforgettable brush with a mountain lion—the horses never once let me down or even gave me a moment's pause. Indeed, as the summer passed, I came to rely more on them—and their relationship with Josh—than on my own judgment. And the knowledge came that the three of them were actually running things and I was just along for the wonderful ride. Again and again as we went into the mountains I relinquished my feeling of individual, my feeling of self, to the three of them; we would start up the mountain out of the yard, and within a few hundred feet the mare—which I habitually rode, using the little black pony for packing—would take over and run the show. Josh would go out ahead on the trail, and if he ran into anything—a moose or an elk or, less frequently, a bear— he would come back and look at the mare, and she would slow and let me come to attention and react. When the ride got long, as it sometimes did, and Josh grew tired (he ran at least six miles for every mile the horse covered) and there was a long flat area, such as a meadow, he would wait until there was a boulder or nearby hummock and would jump up behind me on the mare and ride for a while, sitting on her rump. When—how—they worked this out, I had no idea. I had never seen it before and never since, with other dogs and horses. But they did it, irrespective of me, and as we rode, the seeds for this book were planted. And as they sprouted and grew with note taking and the mining of my childhood memories came the belief, the solid belief, that it is true not just for me but for all of us.

We don't own animals. Even those we kill to eat.

We live with them.

We *get* to live with them.

And so to Corky.

To shorten what many people have come to think of as a kind of madness—indeed, an earlier book of mine terms it a kind of madness—I decided at the age of sixty-seven to go back to dogs and Alaska and run the Iditarod again.

There are/were many reasons for this decision to run it after a lapse of twenty years, but for people with normal lives they do not seem even remotely logical. In many respects I think it is something on the order of combat; for people who have never experienced it, it is impossible to explain except to say it is outrageous, and for people who have done it, no explanation is necessary.

I missed the dogs.

Terribly.

Every day I thought of them: dogs long gone, old friends passed, and the joy and beauty they gave me.

And I missed the wilds of Alaska, to run through and in them with a dog team, alone and silent in such staggering beauty. When I took a friend of mine from Scotland to Alaskan mountains and rivers and forest—this was an articulate, well-read, educated friend—he could only stand, half crying, and say, "Jesus Christ," over and over again in a kind of prayer.

All of that. The wild and the dogs and the stunning joy of dancing through the wilderness with them hung over me—no, danced out ahead of me—every single waking minute of every single waking day.

The hard thing to understand is that I ever left it, that I didn't go back to the dogs sooner. Age didn't seem to matter; nor did physical condition, though everything crazy you do when you're young, every bar fight, every rough horse ridden and thrown from, every torturous twist the military does to your body comes back with a kind of staggering vengeance when you get old. Creaking bones, small and large traveling pains, bad vision . . .

And none of it seemed to matter even remotely; the pain became a kind of wonderful recognition that I was still alive, another obstacle to beat or, as the Marines put it, "Pain is weakness leaving the body." Bushwa, of course, but it was and is that way for me and so I found some sled dogs.

And then more sled dogs.

And still more sled dogs.

And equipment . . .

I bought an old Ford truck with a dog box on it, found a shack in the woods in northern Minnesota, and tried training there. When that didn't work—way too crowded; I waited at a trail intersection one afternoon while one hundred and four snow machines (at least fifty of them were pulling work sleds loaded with cases of beer) passed in front of my lead dog—I cut, as they say, and ran to Alaska, where I found an ugly old house, a kind of huge suburban shack, back in the bush, and sort of moved in.

"Sort of," because there were no facilities for sled dogs. Each dog needed a post driven into the ground, with a chain and an insulated house. I could have kept them on a picket chain while I built the kennel—which would take two months; I would have to rent a bulldozer to clear a place, drill holes, build houses, etc. That seemed excessive, to have them confined to short pickets for all that time.

Luckily, a company would take the dogs to Juneau, put them up on the snow/glaciers for the summer to give rides to tourists, feed them whatever food I wanted to feed them, and in general take really good care of them. Plus they would continue to get healthy exercise.

I agreed to it, drove them to Juneau, watched them take helicopter rides up to the glacier—a singular experience for dogs who have never been off the ground—and came back to a house empty of dogs. It was a strange feeling—as if my family were suddenly gone.

I rented a bulldozer and cleared four acres of the small—if ancient—black spruce and set to work. In Wasilla there was a place where good tools could be rented, and I found a kind of machine for drilling four-foot-deep-by-eight-inch-wide holes in the ground. It was not the small auger type, but a large rig on wheels that made an extraordinary amount of noise and slamming motions while it was running so that it required constant attention and it was impossible to see or hear anything else.

And now a brief note on Alaska. Many people say many mistaken things about the state, people who have never lived there, as if it were a kind of Disneyland of the north, with quaintly "cute" animals like wolves, bears, and moose, which seem to have been placed there somehow for photo opportunities. Those are largely people who never truly get off the bus but shoot pictures through the windows.

The truth is Alaska is for real, and with a lack of knowledge, of understanding, this reality comes with sometimes great and sometimes lethal danger. At the time of this writing, a young woman schoolteacher visiting one of the outlying villages went for a jog—which she was accustomed to doing in the Lower 48—and was dragged down, killed, and eaten by wolves. Bears attack frequently—both black bears and grizzlies—as do moose, which can do great damage by kicking. (They are as strong as horses.) I personally know of several people severely injured by moose and four killed and eaten by bears.

When I moved back up to Alaska, I had in a strange way fallen into the category of the ignorant tourist. I had run two Iditarods, it was true, back in 1983 and 1985, but then I had been just visiting in winter when bears were in hibernation and did not understand or truly know the possibilities of summer attacks by bears.

And I bought a house at the end of a road that terminated on the very edge of a wilderness that stretched for literally thousands of miles. Not a road or village or settlement or power line or even a single person existed in this staggering immensity. Just wild things in the wild.

And I took a bulldozer and cleared four acres and moved in more or less like I owned the place.

Well.

Many things disagreed with me about this so-called ownership. On the first warm day, approximately two hundred million mosquitoes decided to express this disagreement and came to call. Then bears hit my trash, and I think it was a wolverine (there are no skunks in Alaska proper—nor snakes) that sprayed on most of what I had outside. A moose dented the *top* of my truck hood—I think just to be annoying. It was strange because I was alone—my dog handler being with the dogs on the glacier in Juneau—and I kept feeling as though I was being watched.

And I was.

About halfway through the afternoon of the second day with the heavy boring machine slamming me around, I felt a call from nature and I shut the machine down and went into the house to answer that call. I wasn't gone fifteen or twenty minutes, but when I came out, I found I was not alone.

The drilling rig had kicked up a pile of soft dirt next to the hole, and there, in that pile of soft dirt, was a single bear track that measured seven and a half inches wide by eleven and a half inches long.

Grizzly.

Easily twice the size of most black bears.

It had been watching me.

Every hair on the back of my neck stood up.

It had stood there, back in the thick trees—not thirty or forty feet away—and watched me drilling holes. As soon as I'd gone into the house, it had come forward to see what I had been doing—to check out the hole—and I hadn't seen or heard a thing.

I'd had no clue.

The next time, I thought, it could come up behind me while I was running the machine and simply bite my head off. (One of the bear attacks I had heard of ended in just that way—one bite, clean off. Like a guillotine.)

Strangely, it was not the fear of an attack that bothered me as much as the fact that I was alone, some kind of strange dread of that dark band of spruce and that bears, or any other animal, could stand there and watch and I wouldn't know it.

I needed company. Somebody to watch my back. Somebody to give me at least a small warning.

I needed, really, a dog. And all my sled dogs were gone, up on the glacier for the summer.

And a gun.

I needed a dog for company and a gun—which I did not have—for possible protection. It being so complicated to drive across Canada with firearms, I had left my weapons with my son in Minnesota.

A gun was not a problem. Wasilla had several pawn-shops. At one, I purchased a used Mossberg twelve-gauge pump, which held five rounds and had a slightly short-ened barrel. I also bought a box of Magnum full-diameter slugs and another box with Magnum double-ought buck-shot, fifteen thirty-caliber-round balls per shell, each ball a third of an inch in diameter. Either way, slugs or buck-shot, pumping in one after the other, I could pretty much stop a charging Buick.

False security, as we will find later.

As for the dog, I always got my pets at animal shelters, so I called the Wasilla shelter and was told—perfect, really—that they had a three-legged border collie that needed a good home. He would make a great pet and work companion. I had, over the years, saved several border collies and found them to be something just a little better than wonderful—way smarter than me—and I planned for him to stay a house pet after the team came back from the glacier in Juneau.

The rule was first come, first served, and there had been another call on the border collie. So I jumped in my truck and roared the forty miles to Wasilla, then on down near the town of Palmer, slid into the parking lot at the shelter . . .

Just, as it turned out, seven minutes too late.

The other people had come for the border collie. Which was fine—they would give it a good home. I asked the woman at the shelter if she had another dog that might be suitable.

"Well . . . there is one that we just got and can't afford to keep, since it will need a lot of medical and dental care and we don't have any money. . . ."

Oh, I thought. *Good. Medical bills.* "Well, I don't know. I kind of need one pretty quick. . . ."

"He was scheduled to be put down tomorrow if nobody showed for him."

Well. She was probably playing me, but that was all right; you do what you have to do to save a dog, and she was hitting the target perfectly. I could not stand to have a dog put down. In a moment of illogical compassion and perhaps some weakness, I said: "All right. Bring him out."

And so I met Corky. An eight-pound toy poodle covered with abscesses, mouth filled with rotten teeth, one ear and his butt packed with pus. He was probably ten or eleven years old, though the people who dumped him said in a form that he was only six. They also said that the reason they were leaving him was that he was "too rambunctious."

"What did he do?" I asked as they brought him out in the little kennel the people had left him in. "Rip the tires off the car?" How the hell could such a little thing be "too rambunctious"?

There was no way, I thought, that this dog would be able to save me from grizzlies. . . . He'd be lucky to get home alive, judging by the way he looked.

And yet.

And yet there he was, looking at me through sickened, red eyes, wanting something, wanting me to sign, to acknowledge the contract, the age-old contract between a man and a dog, the contract that says simply, "I will be for you if you will be for me. . . ."

I reached out and took him in my arms, and he screamed in pain, screamed all the way to the truck, then curled up in my lap, whimpering, as I took him to the vet, where he screamed as I carried him into her office and left him.

For three days.

After which, having gone through many procedures for draining abscesses, cleaning out infections, pulling rotten teeth, and going through dental surgery (he wound up with only three teeth, the two forward grippers on the bottom and one—right—canine on top), and after I paid a walloping $1,207.94, I had a "free" watch poodle from the pound.

It just couldn't be that he would work out. Eight stomping

pounds of pure poodle—any big bird could carry him off. He will, I thought, turn out to be a live table ornament, something for the cat (named Hero) to bat around and play with. A toy—and indeed, they called them toy poodles.

However, not only was I wrong, completely wrong—damn near dead wrong—but Corky turned out to be perfect, absolutely perfect for the job.

The thing is, in some way he knew—he *knew*—what it was all about. I brought him home and decided that except for letting him go outside for the bathroom, I would keep him in the house. The truth is there were great risks for him outdoors. Bald eagles were always about—sometimes as many as four sitting in trees around the house. There were truly enormous owls—one of which nailed a friend's Pomeranian, carried it off never to be seen again. There were also wolves (I lived on the edge of the famed Talkeetna pack's territory—in reality a series of smaller roaming packs all stemming from the core pack and covering an area as big as some eastern states), fox, and (I think) coyotes, or something near it. All of them would grab a cat or a poodle—the wolves sometimes taking pets as large as Labs and collies, not to mention livestock and now and then a human.

So when I brought him home, I put him in the house and that first morning went into the cleared area, leaned the shotgun against a big rock, fired up the hole digger, and went to work, thinking, if not a good watch dog, he was still a good friend, and I had, if needed, the shotgun.

Strangely, as noisy and as powerful as the beast of a machine was—it dug an eight-inch-by-four-foot-deep hole in virtually no time at all, kicking my tail all the time—it seemed to be breaking down.

There was a new sound coming from it—a high-pitched, keening whine from a bearing (I thought). I swore. Part of the agreement was that though it was a rental, I was responsible for anything that happened to it while I had possession. When it comes to fixing mechanical things, I fell somewhere into the Complete Idiot level. I stopped the machine, thinking I could at least check the oil (which was my limit of repair).

The whining didn't stop with the engine and seemed to be coming from somewhere behind me.

I turned to face the house, and there, in the big window on the ground floor—the sill three feet above the floor—was Corky.

He had somehow jumped up to the sill and was on his back legs on the ledge, clawing at the window with his front feet, screaming in that high-pitched ruined-bearing sound I thought had come from the posthole digger machine.

I smiled and thought how sweet it was; he wanted to be outside with me.

I then noticed something I had not seen initially. He was clawing at the window with a true kind of madness; if it were only affection, I thought, he must really love me, way more than he'd indicated when I'd brought him home from the pound.

The second thing hit me at the same moment. He wasn't looking at me. Instead he was looking off to my right, toward the northwest corner of the cleared area. I turned to see a full-on male grizzly standing just at the edge of the blue spruce, studying me (I thought) like I was a side of beef. I had no idea how long he'd been there—probably as long as the high-pitched whining had been sounding over the bellow of the engine—certainly minutes. Several minutes. And Corky had been trying to warn me.

I knew then very little of bears. I'd heard all the horror stories—many of them true—but I also knew that my neighbor had thrown rocks at a grizzly that was in her garden and it had run off.

I wasn't about to throw a rock at this guy; he was at least eight hundred pounds and taller than me and would probably take the extra time while killing me to insert the rock . . .

But I didn't have to worry, I thought. I had the shotgun. The gun made me superior to almost all living things in North America. It was a massive twelve-gauge Magnum. The gun would solve the problem. I would shoot once

in the air—which everybody said to do—and the bear would leave. I would jack another shell into it just in case he decided to come at me. Simple, really. I had done the army. I knew how to shoot very well—as well as an expert. There was no real problem.

Here is what I would have liked to have happened. I would swing gracefully, even deftly, one hand swiping the shotgun from the rock, pumping the action with a practiced one-hand motion—the way they show off in movies—and putting a slug in the chamber while clicking the safety off in the same motion. Then I'd swoop the barrel up over the bear, squeeze the trigger . . .

And the truth is it might have been something like that except . . .

First the bear moved. I think he was off balance standing upright. He dropped to all fours and then stood again to gain a new balance. He didn't come toward me at all, but the sudden motion startled me—I might say frightened me—so that I turned too fast and fell flat on my face, my hand outstretched for the shotgun, which I accidently knocked off the rock out of reach.

I scrabbled to my hands and knees—and "scrabbled" is the right word, like a great crab. Somehow I got to the shotgun, and with something between groping and grasping, I managed to get the thing pointed in the general direction of the bear, but way high—I didn't want to hit him. I worked the pump frantically, so that two rounds ejected out and onto the ground unfired. I aimed still higher and squeezed the trigger.

Click.

An awful sound. I double-checked the safety. It was off. I worked the pump again, recocked the piece, calmer now, the bear looking at me with more interest, aimed off to the right of the bear with more care now and squeezed the trigger.

Click.

I felt this wave of soft nausea pass over me. I wasn't really terrified. The bear still stood there; it wasn't charging. Corky was still clawing at the window. In fact, I was relatively calm, although, as I've had happen before in life, several of the glands in my body were beginning to send more and more urgent signals; there was a copper taste in my mouth and definite poop-and-flee information going from my brain to my bottom.

I stood slowly and without making eye contact—not a problem as the bear was still almost fifty yards away—and moved slowly toward the back door of the house.

The bear dropped to all fours—stopping my breath momentarily and nearly stopping my heart—made a loud "whuffing" sound, then turned and disappeared into the woods.

Rule one, I thought. The temperature was cool, but I was covered in sweat, my hands shaking. Rule one: Always test fire a new weapon, no matter how proficient you might think you are.

And rule two: Listen to the poodle.

I went into the house, where Corky greeted me, still in that wonderful high-pitched scream, and we sat for a time in a big chair, Corky in my lap, me petting him and telling him that even with me spending more than a thousand dollars on him, he had been a wonderful buy.

And again he knew. He *knew* what he had done and what his job was, and with each day his work evolved more and more.

From that day forward, for the rest of the summer, we were inseparable. I would awaken at four in the morning, have a bowl of oatmeal, and give Corky his breakfast of raw meat (I had learned years earlier that the best dog food in the world was plain, raw hamburger, no matter the breed), and we would go to work. I bought a new shotgun, which I always kept at hand, and the Walmart in Wasilla started carrying an anti-bear spray that was very effective, which I carried in a holster on my belt.

Corky sat at my side, no matter where I worked, watching the surrounding spruce forest, and if anything moved—anything, a branch, a leaf, a limb—he started the keening sound and I would stop what I was doing and investigate where he looked and always, always there was something.

A breeze, a squirrel, a fox, a grouse with chicks, a wolf, a moose, another squirrel, *dozens* of squirrels, a marten, a porcupine, several bears, more moose, once a wolverine . . . always something.

He was like an early-warning radar, always on guard, always alert, and if that was all he did—watch the forest when I was outside—it would have been enough. With practice, I quickly came to believe him, to trust him and his judgment.

But he expanded his duties constantly. At first he was a guard dog—all eight pounds, well, nine and finally ten when the raw meat kicked in—and then he began to make judgment calls as well. A grouse would take a softer sound than, say, a bear, and in the end a squirrel would be only a whimper while a moose or bear would be an outright bark, with a grizzly bear bringing the loudest bark/scream/whine of all.

I came to depend even more on his knowledge and judgment, to the point that he was no longer my dog, my pet, but we were equals, and finally, as it had been with Josh and the mare, we were not equals any longer but he was above me in some way, able to see what I could not, hear what I could not. We would start out in the morning and I would hesitate at the door, let him out first to look around the yard for a moment, pee on the porch post, declaim the day as useful and safe, and then we would move into it.

And still it grew.

I was sitting at the table one day, having a cup of tea with a friend, Corky sleeping in my lap. The friend had left something he wanted to show me out in his truck and he suddenly stood to walk around me to the door to bring it in. As he moved behind me, Corky awakened, stood on my lap, bared his two lower and one upper-right tooth (a god-awful grotesque look, as if trying to do an Elvis Presley impersonation), and uttered what, for Corky, was a very threatening growl. Considering that Corky knew this friend, loved this friend, had earlier been asleep in this friend's own lap, the growl was surprising, to say the least.

"It's your back," he said. "He doesn't want anybody behind you. . . ."

And that was it. A new criteria to his job—"watch my six," as fighter pilots would put it. Nobody could be behind me without a warning. Not even a friend.

"Thank God he doesn't have opposing thumbs," my friend said. "He'd get a gun and God knows how many people he'd shoot just for walking behind you. . . ."

The thing is, he's not an angry or yappy dog. He loves people, greets them with all the tail wags possible, licks their faces. Absolutely adores children. He's just a loving and sweet dog.

But he's got these rules. His own rules for guarding me, handling me, taking care of me. We are friends. We love each other. He sleeps in bed with me in the crook of my knees, but I am more as well. I am *the job*.

Two more bits of information on Corky. Studies have been done on mirrors and animals, and it has been decided that only primates understand the concept of reflection in a mirror. Even other monkeys don't realize that they're looking at themselves in the reflection.

We have an old 1996 Ford dog truck, which we use for hauling sled dogs. The box in back makes it impossible to see out the back window. But there are large side rear-view mirrors, and Corky watches in the mirrors. When somebody comes up from the rear to pass us, he growls. They're on our six. He reads the mirrors. And nobody, but *nobody*, gets on our six without a warning, because he is, and *knows* he is, after all, the Corkinator. . . .

One further note: The sled dogs came back from the glacier in late September, still before snow, and moved in and peed in their circles and in a wonderful way changed the dynamic of everything. There was glad noise, songs, snarls, and joy, and Corky decided he did not need to patrol the yard from the windows in the house as much as he had. Also, the pandemonium of the kennel scared away the eagles (only for a short time and then they came back with a vengeance, along with thirty ravens—more on this in later chapters), so we could let Corky out in the yard by the house without worrying about air attacks except from owls, which usually hit only at night.

Because of the clamor, he would stay away from the sled dogs. . . .

Or so we thought.

And for a couple of weeks it seemed to be working that way. Because there was no snow, we pulled a four-wheeler with three sixteen-dog teams, strengthening them and training leaders, Corky watching from the windows as we ripped out of the kennel and into the trail system.

Everything seemed to have settled in. There was a bit of extra noise when the sled dogs saw me let Corky out for a few minutes to (I thought) mark the porch posts. I left him there on the front porch in the dark as I went in and started coffee and some bacon for sandwiches, and when I came back to the door, Corky would be sitting there waiting, would come into the house to sit on the windowsill, watch us harness and leave.

The perfect house dog.

Then we got a new inch of snow and I could see tracks, and I found that Corky had hidden issues.

I thought he was peeing on and marking the porch. Dead wrong. His ego was much too substantial for such limited territory. His little poodle tracks—remember, he weighed between eight and ten pounds and most of the sled dogs clocked in at fifty or so—trotted past the porch posts, out around the house directly up to the lead dog position in the kennel (there were two female leaders and one male), and he claimed them, peeing on the edges of their circles, which lit them up, set them to lunging and snarling at him.

He owned them—that's what he was saying with his actions. *You're mine.* Then, dividing the kennel into four more sections, he marked five more places, essentially claiming ownership and leadership over the entire kennel: all eight romping stomping pounds of him. Grizzlies, sled dogs, people—it didn't matter. He owned them all. He simply had no fear.

Then back to the house, touching up the porch post as he came to the door, up the steps, to sit, waiting for me to let him in for breakfast.

We feed pure meat to the sled dogs—well, all dogs, as far as that goes, cut-up chunks of bloody beef heart. And the smell went out and out into the surrounding forest, and drawn by the smell, the eagles came back, started trying to steal it from the sled dogs. Some of their passes and strikes came close to Corky, so we retired him to New Mexico, where I have a shack in the mountains.

I am sitting there now, writing this, and Corky is with me. He is older now, his hearing dampened a bit, his eyes dimming a little, but yesterday I was sitting writing and a flock of wild turkeys (I think about twenty of them) came up onto the back porch, looking for scraps, and Corky hit the glass of the back door like a snarling banshee, shoulder hair up, three teeth bared in slavering-spit Elvis grimace, and he scared them away in a showering storm of turkey poop and blown wing feathers.

My six is still covered.

CHAPTER TWO

A Very Young Soldier, a Very Old
Man, a Mynah Bird Named Betty,
Nuclear War, and Gretchen

1959.

It was difficult, almost impossible, to bridge the age/time
gap between us.

I was eighteen, so young my brain had hardly started
to function; in the army, stationed at Fort Bliss, Texas,
near El Paso, learning to kill my fellow man with various weapons, including missiles and nuclear warheads—
living in a state of perpetual confusion mixed with a dosage
of fear. We expected Russia to attack at any moment—
and we found later that Russia felt the same way about
us. I had without any choice been enrolled in the army's
nuclear-warhead school and had been stunned to learn
the truth about all-out nuclear war; to wit, nobody walks

away, and it doesn't do any good to duck under your desk and hide, as we had been told by the media and in school.

The man sitting across from me at an oilcloth-covered kitchen table was eighty-three. He had lived in the desert his whole life, indeed, what amounted to several lifetimes in many cultures, and he was so sun blasted and deeply wrinkled that it was easy to imagine the wrinkles going all the way through his head to meet in the middle.

Mr. Winnike.

Pronounced Win´-uh-kee.

And in truth I knew little about him. He reached across the table and poured a black substance he claimed was coffee from a stained old enamel pot and smiled, a flash of incredibly white dentures in the old, brown leather face.

"You're here about Gretchen," he said, the voice surprisingly strong, vibrant, almost young. "Everybody wants to know about Gretchen."

I wasn't sure exactly what he was talking about and shrugged. "I don't know a Gretchen. . . ."

"The dog," he said. "You want to know about the dog. Her name is Gretchen."

"Ahh." I nodded. "Yes. I want to know about Gretchen. . . ."

"I knew you would come. The moment we met. Your eyes have dog in them."

I did not know what he meant then—I do now, as I

have learned to know now—but I knew when I met him that he had some . . . some large knowledge about dogs and other animals, and maybe about life, that I wanted to understand.

I remember when I met him.

It had been at a Christmas party. Some family with an immense house—one floor, thirty-four or -five rooms around a Spanish-style courtyard—had invited soldiers from Fort Bliss to come for a Christmas party and dinner. It was a nice gesture, and some of us who were particularly not military in our thinking and on the raw edge of an abyss of too much open military knowledge were glad of the chance to get away from Fort Bliss and get non–mess-hall food.

There had been some drinking, though not much, but at that time in my life I did not drink at all, and as that part of the party grew, I wandered off around the courtyard into some other rooms that were open. In one of them there came a sound like a crowd of people talking, screaming, and jabbering, and I went in to see what was going on.

It was a strange, rather small room with large potted plants—some of them floor to ceiling. I'd started to turn and leave when I heard the sound again; it was muted, as though far off, but it sounded like a large crowd, the kind you see on the street in a political rally or a car race.

But it was inside the room, and curious, I stepped back inside and closed the door, or tried to close it. I felt a body come against it, and when it opened again, an old man entered. He had gone beyond where I—being just eighteen—could measure age. Deep-set wrinkles, bright blue eyes that (and I know it's cliché) twinkled, bald, with an impossibly white denture-flash smile.

"Oh," I said. "Excuse me."

"No problem." He moved past me. "I heard Betty. He's about to start the speech segment of his performance and I like to hear him speak. . . ."

Betty, I thought, and *him speak*. Well, I decided, he's obviously old. I had an uncle in Minnesota who would have conversations with himself, start to finish, and maybe this old gentleman . . .

"I'm sorry," he said. "You haven't been here before, have you?"

"No, sir." There was something about him that made you want to call him "sir." Some firm but gentle dignity.

"So you haven't got a single idea what I'm talking about, do you?"

"No, sir."

"Come here." He moved to a back corner, beneath what looked like a kind of rubber plant, and pointed out a birdcage, which I hadn't seen before. It was a large cage—perhaps four feet high—and inside was a strange-looking bird: black, as big as a small crow, but with stripes of color on its side.

"This is Betty," he said. "He's a mynah bird. Oh, and I'm Winnike. Here's my card."

He handed me a plain card, on which it said, simply, GEORGE WINNIKE, TRAINER, with an address out near the border in Zaragoza. I put the card in my pocket and pointed to the bird. "I don't understand. . . ."

"Oh. He heard the crowd out there, the Christmas guests, and it triggers him to answer with his version of a crowd scene."

"That was her—him? That whole muffled-crowd sound?"

He nodded. "Traffic noise and all. It's the only crowd scene he knows, so he uses it to answer whenever he hears a crowd. You know, to get somebody in here to pay attention to him." He turned to the bird. "Hello, Betty. You're a pretty bird."

"I know," the bird said. "Betty is a pretty bird, sooooo pretty." Then he lapsed back into the crowd sounds. I could have sworn I was listening to a large crowd outside the house. Then he hesitated. The crowd seemed to quiet down, and the next thing I heard, clearly, was the voice of the president giving a speech.

"Seriously?" I asked Mr. Winnike. "President Kennedy?"

"Perfect, isn't it? Sounds just like him. He's giving a campaign speech at some factory—I've never figured out which one it was—but it sounds just like him, doesn't it?"

Questions, I thought. *I have all these questions.* "What . . . ? I mean how . . . ? Why do you call him Betty? I mean, if it's a boy, why does he have a girl's name . . . ?"

"Simple. When they got the bird they didn't know which sex he was, and the people who gave them Betty said it was a girl named Betty. By the time they found out he was a male, it was too late. He already knew his name, answered to his name. So they kept it. But that is not the most complicated thing about Betty."

"How is it . . . ? I mean, how can he make the sound of a crowd and the voice of the president . . . ?"

"Again, it's not so strange. He heard it on the radio, or on television. Many birds can mimic sound—parrots, crows, ravens; they make exact replicas of sounds they hear. And even that is not the most interesting thing about Betty. There is still one question left to ask, and it is the most important one."

"What is it?"

"Why . . . ?"

"Why what?"

"Why does Betty want to communicate with us, with people? *Why* is he calling out?"

"He wants to have people come to him?" I said. "He wants people to be with him?"

"And again, *why*?"

I thought of myself, of what had become of me, of how I was after I joined the army. I did not have a family, not really, and the army seemed to be then a very strange place. "Because he's lonely?"

"Lord," Mr. Winnike said, smiling a sigh. "Do you suppose that's it? That's all it is? He's lonely?"

Of course I didn't know, would probably never know— if the experts were right, I would soon be dead, burned in intense white clouds hotter than the sun. Nuclear war, according to them, according to the press, was imminent. The missiles were in Cuba, ready to be fired. Yahoo.

"Perhaps you should come and meet Gretchen; perhaps she can show us. . . ."

And so to Gretchen.

Mr. Winnike—I never called him by his first name, though it was on the card; I never seemed to remember it—lived in a house down along the Mexican border that seemed run-down when I first saw it as I parked in the track that could hardly be called a driveway: two ruts in the sandy dirt that led to a small chain-link gate, which was closed. The house was clapboard, which was strange in this desert country, with faded white paint and a small second story. It was surrounded by a yard that was mostly composed of desert sand, powdered clay dirt, and brush plants on the border that had obviously been hand planted but were so old and withered that God only knew what they were originally. I could not see a leaf anywhere on the dry gray branches.

I parked and let myself in the gate, and as I latched it behind me, I heard a screen door slam open and spring closed and turned to see a metallic-gray streak of a dog screaming toward me from the porch steps.

"It's Gretchen," Mr. Winnike called from the porch. "Don't worry. She's friendly. Just do as she tells you."

A strange thing to say, I thought; how could she tell me

anything? But I stopped, waited, and was surprised to see her slam to a bottom-dragging stop three feet in front of me, eyes bright on my eyes, tongue hanging to the side in a happy smile.

She sat for just a moment, studying me, then raised her right forefoot in a hand-shaking gesture. I nodded, leaned down, and shook hands, whereupon she came around me, tucked into a perfect heel against my left leg, and gently push-nudged me up the porch steps to the screen door. She opened it with her paw and nose and escorted me into the house, where she—again working her shoulder against my left leg—escorted/guided me to one of three chairs at an old kitchen table. She gestured with her nose and a nudge for me to sit down. Mr. Winnike sat at the other end, and I was surprised to see Gretchen climb into the third chair, positioned so she was slightly between us, sitting on the chair with one paw on the table. She sighed then, looked first at me, then at Mr. Winnike, then to the stove.

All without any signals or help or even a sound from Mr. Winnike.

"Would you," he now said softly, returning Gretchen's look at the stove, "like a cup of coffee?"

"Is she—I mean, is that a request from her . . . ?" I stopped, then nodded. "Please. I would like a cup of coffee."

He stood, moved to the stove, where he took the pot and two cups, which he put on the table, one for me and one in front of Gretchen. He poured coffee in both of them, filled his own, which was already on the table, then added cream and sugar from a bowl into his cup before he returned the pot to the stove and sat slowly at the other end of the table.

Gretchen took a short lap of her coffee, surprisingly neat, then looked up at me and with a gentle paw pushed the sugar bowl over toward me.

The coffee was profoundly black, almost tar, and so strong it seemed to jump at me from the cup. I took the

sugar spoon from the bowl and put four spoonfuls in my cup, stirred it, smiled at Gretchen, and nodded. "This is good."

She—and it can only be called this—returned my smile, seemed to nod with satisfaction, looked at Mr. Winnike, then back to me, and back to him, back to me. . . .

"She wants us," Mr. Winnike said, and now he smiled self-consciously, or seemed to, "to have a conversation." He didn't seem embarrassed so much as just reluctant to ask something that on the face of it seemed so singular and odd.

"I see," I said. "A conversation. She wants us to have a conversation. If you're going to tell me that she talks . . ."

"Well, the truth is she *does* talk. Or rather, not really. But when she started to train me . . ."

"She trained *you*?" I stared at him, then at Gretchen. "Dogs don't train people. . . ."

He smiled, as I had read in some book, "not unkindly," and nodded slowly. "I had that same thought when it happened. Dogs, I thought, don't train people. People train dogs. But think now, think of the mynah bird that night at the party. He was making a crowd sound and the presidential speech, remember? He was making the crowd sound for what reason?"

"To attract . . . ," I said. "To attract attention."

He nodded. "From whom?"

"From the people at the party. From us . . ."

"From the people at the party." Mr. Winnike nodded, again smiling, dentures impossibly white. "Whom he had trained to come when he made the crowd sounds."

"But couldn't it be the other way? Couldn't the people have trained him to make crowd sounds so they would come . . . ?"

And I could see it then—see how it didn't work backward, how it could never work backward.

"We think, we all think, people think, man thinks he is superior, always superior, and in truth it is the other way around—dead opposite. Have you ever been to Yellowstone Park? You know, on vacation with your family?"

I shook my head. Boyhood on uncles' farms, in the Philippines for two years, then with drunk abusive parents back in Minnesota until I could run away to the army. To initial training with personal weapons, then more training, school upon technical weapons school when not reassigned, until, finally, and the word was *finally*, the ultimate and all-consuming horror of nuclear-warhead school. And the impending all-destructive war with Russia when we would all—when every single living thing on the planet would be—would be . . . "No. I didn't have that kind of family. You know. Where we took vacations."

He paused a moment, studying me, then nodded. "Well,

if you had, you would have seen the bears working at getting into cars as they drove slowly by on the park highway, getting the food the people in the cars had for them."

"Had been trained," I said, nodding. "That the people in the cars had been trained to bring to feed the bears, the cute bears, the cute wild bears that did what they had to do to train people to bring them food . . ."

"Exactly," he said, nodding again. He paused to take a sip of the tar-black coffee, then hand rolled a cigarette from a small packet of tobacco and wheat-straw papers, which he lit with a large wooden match scratched on the underside of the table. He drew deeply, coughed intensely—it was then that I first truly noticed he had a viciously fluid-sounding persistent cough—and gestured to Gretchen. She had been "watching" the conversation, swiveling her head from one to the other as we spoke— much like watching a tennis match—and I had noticed that now and then, at odd intervals, her ears would perk up and she would seem to almost nod.

"I noticed being trained by Gretchen early on with her, when I first trained her to simply sit." Another drag, which used up the rest of the cigarette so rapidly the red-hot end of it burned back into his fingers. "Although, to be honest about it, I think it had been happening all along with other dogs, horses, and even chickens."

"Chickens?"

"Well," he said, smiling—and it seemed impossible that his dentures could remain so flashing white with all the coffee and cigarettes he consumed. "Maybe just one or two, and a rooster . . ."

He closed his eyes and fought a cough, then opened them but did not look at me. Instead he softened his gaze and passed his eyes over Gretchen, then out the window, out and out, not looking at anything in particular except perhaps a far time and place that didn't exist any longer.

"I have been training animals for a long time," he said at length. "Fifty, sixty years. Dogs for hunting, for working stock, for companions; horses for work and show or just to gentle them. Trained almost every kind of animal that walks or crawls except cats. Not a way to train a cat—they got no give to them. All take. Even trained or half trained a couple of snakes for a fat man who came through El Paso making a movie about snakes. And I know in the end that they all, even the snakes, trained me as well. Think of it— when a rattler sets to buzzing, what's he doing? A kind of talking, a warning—he's training you, teaching you to get away."

He reached now and ran one of Gretchen's soft ears through his gnarled, bent fingers, like silk through barb-wire. "And I never saw it until I started with Gretchen. Got her to sit one day. The same day, she looked a long time at me and at a piece of cookie"—and here she perked up, ears more alert with the word "cookie"—"in my hand, and she saw the cookie and my eyes and then she sat. Clean and down. As much as if she'd said, 'I'll sit and then you give me that piece of cookie,' and she did and I did and it was the first time I knew I had been wrong all along. I never trained one animal. Not once . . ."

"They trained you."

He nodded. "I always got what I wanted, what I needed, or almost always, but it was all working backward and I didn't know it, didn't see it until Gretchen showed me how to see, how to know, how to learn."

Gretchen sat looking at him, into his eyes, as he talked, clearly loving him but more, too, something more. She heard more, felt more in some way, and I realized with a start that she was listening to every word, every single word.

And more—much more—she *understood* some of them.

He had seen my look, and his smile widened and he nodded. "That's why she wants a conversation. When she hears a word she knows, she feels like she's more a part of it."

"How many does she know?"

"I'm not sure. I tried keeping track of them at first and got up to seven hundred or seven hundred and fifty before I lost the thread of it. I think she's way past a thousand now—a thousand words she recognizes and places with some object or place or thought. And she's learning more all the time, just stacking them up. But there's more, too."

I looked at her, thought I was maybe seeing some of kind of a freak—no, miracle. Some kind of miracle. "What could be more than this?"

"She has learned how to understand people in some way that goes with the language. So that you can actually talk to her, or almost talk to her. Watch her. Watch her reaction when you say something she knows and likes. Say the word c.o.o.k.i.e." (He spelled it.)

"Cookie," I said, and there it was; she perked at the word, and (I swear it) seemed to add to it, to almost nod.

Winnike saw it as well and smiled. "She knows the word, of course, and that was the alerting part of it, but that second little bit was because she likes it, wants to eat one." He stood and went to the cabinet over the sink, took a vanilla cookie from a jar, and gave it to her. She ate it with two small, delicate bites, then nodded again and with a half grimace added a toothy look.

"She's smiling," Winnike said. "She picked it up from a little girl who came to visit who kept smiling at her. Now, say something she won't like, wouldn't think of eating. . . ."

"Gretchen," I said. "Would you like some broccoli?"

And here she shook her head in a negative manner, studying me the whole time.

"Now another thing she might like to eat . . ."

"Steak," I said, "smothered in gravy."

She alerted, nodded, then smiled, and he gave her a cookie.

We went back and forth that way for a time—pork chops and spinach, chicken and grapefruit, beef stroganoff and eggplant—and she was right, dead right every time. She would shake her head in a negative way when she didn't like it, nod in a positive way when she did.

"She knows," I said, taking a sip of my coffee; somehow cold it was more palatable than it had been hot. Cold and sticky sweet. Like Kool-Aid from the devil. "She knows all the words. How is that . . . ? Is that even possible?"

He shook his head. "It's not that. I doubt even all humans would know all the words. It's the other thing, the thing that surprised me and led me away from my former life. What I thought I knew my whole life . . ."

"What was that?"

"She 'reads' people. . . ."

"I don't know what that means."

"I'm not sure I do, either. But I think she can tell by voice or posture or smell or some thought wave, or some-*thing*, when a person is saying a food she wouldn't want to eat, or when he says something she would like. . . ."

"But how could she know . . . me? We've never met. How would she know anything about me, about my speech or posture or smell? How could she know anything about me?"

He nodded. "I understand and agree with your thinking, or how I believe you're thinking. But the thing is, it's not just you. I've had other people in here, old people, young people, children barely old enough to understand what I mean, and they're all the same. She reads them all. . . ."

"She's reading their minds?" I shook my head. "You think she's actually reading their minds?"

He hesitated, sighed, rolled another cigarette, and poured more coffee—in my cup as well as in his—before I could stop him. I wouldn't be able to sleep for the rest of my life. "No. Yes. Maybe. God, *I* don't know. But I have *seen* it and know what I've *seen*. The only way I think I can understand it, or feel that I know what she's doing, is I have to think in some kind of way that I don't really believe in—spirits and vapor clouds or thought beams or some of that other kind of wild stuff. Thing is, thing is, I'm just an old cowboy who took to training animals and don't know how that other kind of thing works. Do you?"

I shook my head briefly, then thought of the school I was going to with blast patterns and radioactive winds and radiation lobes and flash damage with melted people who were turned into instantaneous shadows on concrete. He could not know any of this, would probably not understand it any better than I understood what I was see-ing with Gretchen. "No, not really."

"Is it"—he sighed—"would it be something you might like to learn, to know?"

I looked at Gretchen. She looked up at me, waiting, waiting, waiting for, for what?

For me?

For me.

"Yes. On the weekends when I'm not at school. I can come each weekend, if that's all right?"

He nodded, and so it was that I came to talk to Gretchen and listen to Gretchen, and Gretchen kept me from going insane—or something like it.

The thing was, I didn't know what I was seeing or hear-ing. I decided to take a notebook and simply write down words or subjects she liked or disliked and see if there was a pattern.

Again:

"Broccoli"—head shake negative.

"Steak"—head moved in nod.

"Turnip"—negative.

"Butter"—positive.

"Butter" in negative tone—positive.

"Spinach" in positive tone—negative.

Here—and almost in a regular rhythm—she would stop for a sip, or a couple of laps of coffee, a tail wag, and (infrequently) the need to go outside and relieve herself, to return quickly, get back up in the chair to look at me quizzically, head cocked, waiting for the next question.

No matter what I tried, I could not confuse her, catch her out. I changed tone of voice, facial expression, gesturing with hands, *not* gesturing with hands. Always she would give the correct, or what I assumed to be the correct, answer.

"Pork chop" in angry tone—positive.

"Ice cream" in anger—positive.

"Vinegar" in loving tone—negative.

I sat in the chair backward, watching her with a small mirror I found in an amazingly decrepit bathroom, and she never missed.

"Jackrabbit running fast," my back to Gretchen—positive.

"Bowl of okra," my back to Gretchen, positive voice—negative response with a small shake of the head and a courteous tail wag.

"Oatmeal, no condiment," negative tone—positive nod.

Oatmeal, brown sugar and butter on top," negative tone—positive nod.

And slowly, over three or four or five weekends, it became evident that she was somehow "reading" me, and it was still more evident in another short time that she had begun testing me, seeing what I "knew" or could be taught.

One cold November morning, at least cold for El Paso, I drove down along the river in my old 1951 Buick (army pay then wasn't what it is now; I made $82.50 a month and was forced to pay 10 percent back in donations to United Fund) that barely ran. I had paid seventy-four dollars for the car, and it was worth that—or nearly.

Inside, the old house was warm—a small potbellied stove in the corner burned a cherry red with mesquite—and Gretchen met me outside as she always did. Mr. Winnike was gone, but he had left a pot of coffee. God, it was so strong. I still remember the bite of that first sip; it was worse even than army coffee, which was nearly brain damaging. I sat at the table, jolted awake by the coffee, petted Gretchen on top of her domed head, got a tail wag and, in as positive a tone as possible, said: "Used motor oil."

And got no response at all. The first time. Clearly it was something she wouldn't like to eat—and most of these decision-questions involved food. Or smell. Or noise.

And here nothing.

Then I noticed something.

In front of her, on the table, was a small piece of prickly pear cactus, just a corner of a tiny lobe, big enough to have a couple of spines sticking out of it. I hadn't seen her bring it in, and for moment I thought it must have stuck to her ear and flopped on the table. I reached to brush it off the table, and she stopped me with her nose, looked pointedly at the cactus, and gave a deliberate negative shake of her head, then looked up at me.

"You don't like cactus?" I said.

Again, a negative shake, then a focused study of my face, waiting.

Waiting.

Waiting.

For what?

Me. A response. I looked at the cactus, saw the needle-sharp spines, and agreed wholeheartedly that I didn't like that piece of cactus either. I shook my head in a negative.

Bang. She got rid of the cactus—put it by the door—and picked up a small stick. She put it on the table, looked up at me and nodded, waiting, I returned the nod, reached for the stick, thinking she wanted me to throw it, but before I could pick it up, she grabbed it and was out the door.

We were not to play. We were working, studying, thinking.

Learning.

And so that day passed. Not with me testing her but the opposite. She was finding out what I knew, what I thought, and somewhere in that day, I realized with a kind of shock, or stunned belief, that we were actually "talking."

I had, as a small child, been raised by my grandmother—a wonderful, all-knowing woman brought up on farms in Norway and later in northern Minnesota. She believed in the old Norse tales of gods and goddesses and spirits of another world, another spirit world that could and often did talk through animals, telling tales of love and hate and joy and music. Sometimes when birds were singing, she would put her hand on my arm and say, "Songs, for you and me, from them; the birds sing for them, for us. . . ."

I did not disbelieve it, actually, but simply thought it was something perhaps only old people could know, a code I did not understand yet. Like when it was going to rain or snow or when somebody would be close to death or birth. I was not skeptical so much as blank, unable to understand.

But now it was true for me, and open, and clear. Gretchen was, in her way, a very real way, bringing me into a conversation; she knew many things I liked, and now she was showing me some of the things she liked and disliked. We were very definitely "talking," and as the afternoon drew on, my level of astonishment grew lower and I accepted it and began to understand what I was really doing:

Having a conversation with a friend.

We had—or rather Gretchen had—found a way to break down the communication barrier and interlock with another species. It was simple, clean, and very elegant— we looked at things, said what we thought of them, and with more depth than I thought possible, we understood each other completely.

It was, in many ways, for me a lifesaving understanding. I had come to the army as an escape from my life—as many men did, I suppose—and though I'd had a complex and rougher childhood than most, I was still virtually unsophisticated. I had seen many ugly things as a child in the Philippines, when the war with Japan was still not quite finished, and through the hazy viewfinder of alcoholic parents, but as the real world hit me, I was simply not able to handle it.

Because I had a semi-technical background in high school, the army started putting me through various electronic-weapons schools: missiles, both antiaircraft and surface-to-surface tactical weapons, which included the care, maintenance, and firing of nuclear weapons, and so to nuclear-warhead schools.

At that time—and in many ways it is still true—the public was given at best a very limited and horribly skewed idea of what nuclear war would be like. True, we had dropped two nuclear weapons (designated then as atomic bombs) on Japan—one on a city called Hiroshima and another on a city named Nagasaki. They were devastating and primarily leveled both cities, but little was told to the public then except that a new kind of bomb had been used against the Japanese. Soon Russia also had the bomb and the Cold War started. We rushed to the edge of nuclear war, and a kind of mass panic hit the United States, with people building bomb shelters and leaving to live in isolated parts of the world in sophisticated bunkers where they thought they might be safe.

But little was told accurately about how the weapons actually worked, and much that was said was so wrong as to be dangerous and downright silly.

In public school we were told to hide under our desks, or duck on the lawn and cover ourselves with our jackets, or hide along a wall with our hands over our heads.

It was so incorrect, so inane, as to be criminal, and when the army sent me to nuclear-warhead school, I had absolutely no idea of what to expect, of the reality of this new kind of tech war. I was brought to a shattering of my ignorance almost as brutal as the weapons themselves.

We sat at desks, with notebooks, the first day of the class. While most of the classes we took were taught by soldiers and sometimes ex-soldiers who were tech reps, in this case a civilian walked into the room. He sat on the edge of a desk, lit a cigarette (we were ourselves not allowed to smoke except in outside breaks), smiled in an almost deprecating way, and said:

"When the atomic bomb was dropped on Hiroshima, it killed between eighty-five thousand and one hundred and twenty thousand people in three hundredths of a second. The human brain operates on a much slower frequency than that speed, and so therefore they were vaporized—reduced to less than their base molecular or carbon level—faster than they could think about it, faster than they could know. They would have had no cognizance of their own death, would simply not mentally know they had been killed, had died, or had ever lived—nothing into nothingness." He took a drag off the cigarette. "The yield of that warhead was the same as approximately twenty thousand tons of conventional explosive, and essentially the same for the warhead dropped on Nagasaki, with the same results. It is important for you to know now that in current terms, these are actually incredibly small warheads, and indeed, are primarily used as triggers for larger-yield weapons, weapons with millions of tons of yield, numbers that are almost literally unimaginable."

But I was gone, stuck on the fact that hundreds of thousands—even millions of people, with the more advanced weapons—could be killed without knowing it, could simply be evaporated into nothingness without knowing that it had happened.

Was it, then, I thought, like they had never existed at all? In their own minds? Simply never have *been*?

It was then—half a century ago—illegal to speak to anyone about any of this, so I bottled it up, but I could not stop thinking of it, the horror of it, knowing what practically nobody else could know; I was eighteen years old and stuck with such insane knowledge.

And then I met Gretchen and so to sanity; I could speak to nobody else, no human, and so I spoke to Gretchen.

On weekends when Mr. Winnike was not there, I would sit and have coffee with her—I must confess that I made it somewhat weaker than he would have done and that she was often negative about how I made it, lapping a bit and then shaking her head slowly from side to side. But she was too courteous to be outright rude and accepted my effort.

The talks went on for three or four weekends with me discussing various nuclear yields and how the bombs worked and frankly how insane it all was, and she was so kind to me. I mean she was very negative about the whole thing, shaking her head from side to side; she did not approve of the use of nuclear tactical weapons at all. But in some way, she was gentle with me at the same time.

We became closer and closer, and when she could sense my sincere frustration growing to an uncomfortable level, she would pause and go outside and bring me something positive from her own life—a favorite stick, a stuffed or rubber toy—which she would place on the table in front of me, pushing it slowly to me with her paw . . . an easing thing, a gentling touch.

I had many dogs before knowing her, and Lord knows how many dogs have wonderfully entered my life in the past fifty years since I met her. But the way she helped me—as no human, really, could have helped me—by breaking down the interspecies interlock and letting her mind come into my thinking . . . There was such care, such love.

Soon after this I was sent once more to Fort Sill, Oklahoma, for still more missile and radar schooling. I was gone, without seeing her, for seven months. When I came back, Mr. Winnike—doubtless due to the coffee— had passed away. When I went to see him and Gretchen, the house was empty and the neighbor lady told me that when he died, Gretchen had come to her house and all but dragged her back for help but it was too late. Soon after, his family had come and taken her back to the Houston area, where they lived.

I wrote to them (this was half a century before the Internet or e-mail) and they informed me that not long after she had come to live with them, their three-year-old daughter had nearly stepped on a diamondback rattlesnake in the backyard, but Gretchen had thrown herself between the snake and the little girl and had taken the strike on her shoulder.

It had been a large snake—as many of the rattlers in eastern Texas seem to be—and a solid direct strike. Such a bite would often have enough venom to be fatal. But the family found a vet with antivenom serum (it was new at the time and apparently they had *all* the neighbors and *all* the police calling *all* the people they could to locate the serum), and Gretchen, after a few days of scaring everybody, made a full recovery.

I never saw her again, though I wrote now and then to the people who lived with her. I have never forgotten her, nor will I, and I think she had a full and wonderful life.

I often think of her and see her sitting at that old kitchen table with the oilcloth cover and thick, thick black coffee in a stained cup, which she loved, and I smile when I think of what she would do if I made my voice as positive as possible and said softly, "Snake."

A soft negative movement, left to right, and then her paw pushing something positive, like the small red ball she loved so much, across the table to me.

· CHAPTER THREE ·

Hollywood and the Woman/Dog
Who Knew Hemingway; Then
Four Hundred Sheep and Floating
Louise and the Coyote That Made
Louise Hate Me

—————◆—————

My life turned to Hollywood oddly enough, and it proved a strange place to live and a surprising place to run into an animal that could and did change my life.

And yet . . .

I came to Hollywood from the north woods by way of having been a farm worker and a soldier and working in aerospace as a field engineer—none of which prepared me for what could only be called the madness of the natural workaday world of Hollywood.

Consider: I went from helping to design and track satellites with huge dish antenna at a take-home pay of five hundred dollars a *week* to proofreading (the only job I could get) articles in so-called men's magazines on what kind of car you could drive that would "help to favorably impress the ladies," along with articles on what kind of clothes to wear, what kind of hair color to use, what kind of toothpaste to brush with, what kind of cigarette lighter to use, what kind of food to order in restaurants, what films to see, what films to talk about, how to talk about them (the whole James Bond craze was starting then), when to talk about them, and why to talk about them. . . .

For two hundred and eighty dollars a *month*.

It's what I thought I had to do to learn to write, or at least to make a start, so I found a tiny apartment for two hundred dollars a month—which left eighty a month for food, water, air, and any and all other necessities—and went to work. I read god-awful, horribly misspelled articles (this was long before computers or spell-checkers came onto the scene) until my eyes nearly bled while trying to learn to write at night with the help of three editors. ("Start," said Dick Ashby, a wonderful old editor who worked slowly with me, "with a simple declarative sentence. Then do another. And another. Soon you have a book.")

It was something close to a living nightmare. I swear I had roaches that I had to ask permission from to use the bathroom and/or the kitchen. And to add to the misery, they were my only company.

A month went by, then another dragging, roach-filled, red-eyed month, head swimming from working each night until I passed out, having my work torn apart by the three men the next day, cycling endlessly, it seemed, rolling from office to grungy home back to office. . . .

Until finally Ray Locke (who wrote screenplays and gentle Southern-based stories when he wasn't editing and teaching me) took pity on me and invited me to a small party at his home, where I met Brette Howard (who called herself Lady Brette). . . .

And Faulkner.

Lady Brette was old, ancient, or so it seemed to me, with gray hair losing its battle with age and gimlet-looking eyes that showed she was nearly blind through glasses so thick they could almost have been made with the proverbial Coke-bottle bottoms. Bent in every conceivable way by time, she had two things that fought the age: absolutely perfect white teeth that flashed from the wrinkled old face like beacons of youth and a voice that was so beautiful, soft, low, and Southern, it seemed to have been dipped in honey.

Though she was very old, the teeth and the voice made her beautiful in some wonderful way. I met her sitting in a corner of Ray's living room, sipping some kind of amber drink and petting a small dog in her lap.

"Hello," she said. "The dog's name is Faulkner. . . ."

I told her my name. I was completely enchanted by her but in a strange way, as if there was something about her I would never understand but would always think about, always remember, always want to tell people. The dog was small, curly-haired, and it occupied her lap rather than sat in it. "After the writer," I said. "The dog—his name."

She nodded. "A small joke," she said. "I knew him and helped him to work on a story called *The Reivers*."

"You help writers?"

She shook her head. "Not all. Just the weak ones. I knew Hemingway as well."

"Did you help him?"

"No. He was too hard-boiled and had a bad future coming. . . ."

"How did you know that?"

"Faulkner," she said, smiling. "The dog, I mean. He's psychic. He knows things. Sometimes I think he knows all things. . . ."

"But how does he communicate? Does he speak?" The overall bluntness of much of my life, the enforced reality of it, kept me from completely believing in things like psychic abilities, especially those from animals or other possible fairy tales. Still, I knew there were things beyond anything I understood, and I was not completely negative.

"He speaks to me with his eyes, body language. We have been together all his life, and so we know . . . We know each other so well."

"Does he say anything about me?"

She hesitated for a moment and then said, "You will never be satisfied or content, and a girl or a woman named Gretchen wants to speak with you about steak, and soon you will take a long trip to a place that smells truly awful."

Like that. Just rattled it out. Not to speak or argue about it or even discuss it, just let it come and then dropped it, and it floored me completely. I didn't know about the being happy or content part, but she couldn't possibly have known about Gretchen unless she or the dog were truly gifted, and I didn't find out about the stinky place until later that night, when I got a call from a half uncle named Art who had a sheep farm/ranch in northern Minnesota. He had four hundred ewes due to lamb. Most of them threw twins, some triplets, and his problem came because he had gotten last year's wool bonus check, and it seemed that it was the same amount of money that they wanted for "one of them new Chrysler automobile cars."

And so he bought a new car.

A new Chrysler automobile car.

That had a circular speed-oh-meter (as he put it) that went all the way around to one hundred miles in a single hour.

One hundred miles an hour.

So he had to try it, and at eighty-seven miles an hour the Chrysler decided to abandon the road in favor of a small curve in the Necktie River, where it flipped end for end, cleanly breaking Art's back and throwing him clear before sinking in about twelve feet of stinking mud and sludge locally called turtle poop.

He was calling now from a circular-frame hospital bed in his small living room, where he had to reside for the next couple of months, and would I please come and help him get through lambing?

The long trip. From Hollywood to northern Minnesota.

The stinky place: Nothing smells like a sheep barn with four or five hundred sheep crammed in. The waste turns to raw ammonia, which blinds you and almost literally rips your nose off your face.

Faulkner and Brette were dead right.

And so it was; I flew from Los Angeles to Bemidji, Minnesota, and Art sent an old man named Louie—older than weather, older than dirt—the forty miles to pick me up at the airport in an ancient truck, and in two days I was in the middle of lambing.

Somewhere, in some time long ago—wild sheep living on wild pastures with wild rams breeding wild ewes—there must have been tough, wild lambs being born, where mothers protected lambs, *could* protect their offspring and shelter them and teach them to live. . . .

Then man took over with genetic-breeding concepts and altered the animal to produce more and more wool, thicker and fatter meat, and virtually no brain at all, and the upshot is what we have now: ewes that have to be almost literally hand carried through lambing, coddled and sheltered, or many of them would simply walk away from the lamb when it was born.

The end result is that lambing on any sizable farm or ranch is a twenty-four-hour-a-day job, sleeping in your clothes, grabbing a sandwich now and then, dozing standing in a corner or lying on straw and hoping it is free of sheep urine and manure. Which it usually isn't.

Art had a system that he had worked out over the many years he had been farming, and while it was relatively simple, it still demanded a staggering amount of stamina.

It was spring, late March, with alternately cold and wet weather—now and then a chance of light snow. The sheep—there were four hundred and fifty or so—were kept outside in a small forest-sheltered pasture to the rear of a large metal barn. The barn was divided into twelve smaller pens, each with a thick layer of fresh straw for them to bed in.

The problem with the sheep was that in the shock and pain of birthing, if she was left in the herd, she would often lose track of her lamb and the lamb would die.

So a twenty-four-hour watch was kept on them by sitting outside under the eaves of the barn, and when a ewe began to go into labor, she was quickly taken into the barn and put in the first pen, alone, where she would have her lamb and be left with it for a day or two. Then she would be moved to the next pen, with one or two other ewes and their lambs and then a third pen with five or six ewes, so in the end she knew her own lamb even in a crowd of them.

That's if everything went smoothly.

If, however, things got out of hand—say, a ewe died or couldn't feed her lamb or didn't *want* to feed her lamb, or the lamb died or didn't *want* to nurse on the ewe—then a can of cheap hair spray would be sprayed on the lamb's back and squirted into the ewe's nostrils so she would smell the odor and *think* it was her lamb, and the new pair had to be watched continuously for two or three days to make sure it all worked *while* watching outside for the next ewe going into labor *while* moving them from pen to pen *while* not sleeping or resting. . . .

It was, very nearly, physically impossible. True, Art had an old and very experienced man—Louie—to help him, although Louie was so shattered and warped by arthritis that he could barely move and kept going in and out of a kind of semi-senility when he became exhausted. He would watch and know precisely when a ewe was starting labor—had a wonderful knowledge of sheep—but could barely move. And then Art had me—eager, enthusiastic, willing to help but with energy more like a chicken with its head cut off. Louie would point at a ewe, and I would streak out to bring her into the barn—except that they all looked alike, and in the dark or soft rain I would get the wrong one and frequently get dragged on my face in the muck for my effort.

Had it been just the two of us with the flock, I am sure it would have been a complete disaster. But Louie came with a helper, partner, friend, second brain: a border collie named (he must have wanted the similarities in names)

Louise, and she quickly—after watching me for a moment and seeing how useless I was—took over completely.

When I first saw Louise she seemed to be floating about two feet off the ground, levitating. Louie brought me from the airport and I changed clothes in Art's house, admired his bed (he was very proud of it), and went to the barn, where the sheep were beginning their cycle. Louie, in broken English (he had about a ten-ton Scandinavian accent) had tried to explain the procedure to me as we drove from the airport, but most of what I heard was: "Ven dey cam to sick ve bring dem into barns."

As soon as I was dressed in old clothes, Louie dragged me to the back of the barn and we settled in to watch.

Except . . .

I was seeing things.

It was a misty, cold evening, just dark, with a heavy low-lying fog, and even with the light on the back of the barn, it was impossible to see anything. More correctly, impossible to see any *sheep*.

Instead, floating about two and a half feet off the ground, lying wrapped in a tight little ball with her nose tucked under her tail, was a small black-and-white border collie—dozing in midair. Before I could say anything, she stood—still in midair—took a step to the side, and dropped, vanishing down into the fog. Seconds later she came to the barn door, pushing a reluctant ewe who was starting labor. Once she delivered the ewe, she took a step away from me, hopped up onto the nearest sheep, and ran back across the backs of the ewes, jumping sheep to sheep until she was about in the center of the flock, where she sat—apparently in midair—carefully watching around her for the next sheep.

It was all so cooperative. She sat on the sheep, or, if she felt like resting, actually lay on them, curled in a ball, watching—or, I think in reality "sensing" (I don't see how she could have actually seen them in the fog)—the sheep until one started labor. They didn't seem to mind

her being up there. Indeed, they almost seemed to like it, pushing together to make a more firm bed when she lay down, and if I meddled and tried to get out there and drag a ewe in from the pen, Louise would straighten me out by pushing me away with her shoulder and taking over.

My job was soon relegated to working in the pens, moving the sheep from one to the next to let them learn to recognize their lambs before it got more crowded. I was little more than a clerk, and that was fine, and Louise and Louie and I worked those sheep and got into a rhythm so that Louise was doing all the work and we just supported her. It was like a dance, a dance in the stink of sheep and the smell of newborn steam coming off the lambs and the sounds of them, mothers and lambs, finding one another and love.

And it seemed that it would go on or had gone on forever and that there had always been sheep and lambs and birth.

And then the coyote came.

At first I thought it was a wolf. They were coming back from having been hunted down for bounties, but as she came in the dark and I turned on the lights in the back of the barn, I could see that it was a large coyote. I would find later she was a female.

She hit the back of the flock, tearing ears and udders, indiscriminate and savage, throats, stomachs, rear ends, disabling six or seven sheep in less than two or three minutes—a horrible attack. Louise tried to intervene, but the coyote shouldered her aside, tore at her neck, and went back to the sheep. It is not politically correct but true that I had seen and heard of single coyotes or wolves killing forty sheep in one night without eating any of them.

Art had a gun, a pre–Second World War surplus clunker of a thing, which he kept in the barn. I grabbed it, swung it up, swore at the sights on it, which were rusted and crude, saw the coyote in the dim light, mixed with sheep and Louise, and took quick aim, let the army training kick in. I squeezed one round off and heard:

Thwock, tick! Two hits. *God*, I thought, *not Louise. Please, God, not her.*

And it wasn't. She had gone right when I fired slightly to the left, and I caught the coyote fair in the front of her neck, killing her almost instantly. The bullet had gone cleanly through and struck a ewe in the backbone, killing her almost as fast as the coyote.

I ran from the barn out through the herd to make certain and saw that the coyote was really dead, as was the sheep, but I ran smack into what makes border collies the incredible beings that they are.

Louise grabbed at the coyote's neck, growling, and having made certain that it was dead, tried to bring the sheep back to life. She pulled at the ewe, trying to lift her to her feet, nudged at her ribs in a kind of crude CPR, smelled for the dead ewe's breath, found none, went back to CPR, and when that failed, started dragging the ewe to the barn, where Louie was emerging.

I leaned down and grabbed at the ewe's leg to help, thinking that possibly we could save the lamb, but Louise would have none of it. She looked at me, at the rifle, growled, bared her teeth at me, at the rifle. She seemed to blame us both and was not about to forgive either one of us—me or the rifle.

Ever.

The spring, and lambing, wore on and on for two, three, four more weeks with no sleep and Louie watching and Louise sleeping on the herd and me moving animals from pen to pen. When there was a moment's rest, I would try to pet Louise, but she never allowed me close again, would dismiss me with a soft growl and a push with her nose or shoulder.

I had done a bad thing. I had done the worst thing, the very worst thing.

I had killed one of the flock. No. I had killed one of *her* flock.

No matter that it was an accident, no matter that I killed the coyote that was savaging the flock, savaging *her* flock, or that I loved dogs and sheep and all animals except perhaps mosquitoes and wood ticks . . .

I would not be brought back into the fold, into *her* fold, her family. I could be around, could help in the pens, but we could never be close again.

I had gone too far.

And I still miss her.

CHAPTER FOUR

On Birds, and Bees, and Rest Area Non-negotiated Hostile Existence

Much is made of the inability of the wildness of nature to blend into and mix with what man has done to the world. There was an enormous amount of worry involving the Alaska pipeline and caribou and whether or not the pipe would act as an iron barrier and stop the normal migration patterns of the caribou. In that event there was no need for concern. The caribou indeed seemed not to notice the pipeline at all. In truth, in almost all cases of the meeting of the two worlds—wild and so-called civilized—there rarely seems to be much difficulty. I was sitting on the side apron at Los Angeles International Airport some years ago, waiting in a long line of commercial jets, which were roaring and snorting flame, and looked out the side window of the plane and was amazed to see a scruffy coyote stalking an even grubbier-looking jackrabbit in the grass divider between the runways. Neither of them seemed to notice the giant silver beasts around them. I watched the two until we were out of sight, taking off—both still intent on their drama, as oblivious to the planes as if they were alone in the forest primeval.

Nor was that the only evidence that the wild has supplanted the tame. One hot summer desert day, I was riding my horse on the edge of an ancient dry lake bed, slightly higher on the old shoreline, when I looked out to see at some distance—perhaps half a mile—a jackrabbit ripping out across the dusty bed, leaving a dust line like a bone-dry contrail. Behind it, gaining slightly, came two other lines of dust, made by two hungry coyotes, and they were clever enough to work the rabbit from side to side, each of them working out to the edge to keep him from turning, manipulating him toward the center between them, slower and slower until . . .

The rabbit seemed doomed. While prairie jackrabbits are capable of amazing bursts of speed—up to and over fifty miles an hour—they are relatively short-winded. When worked the way this one was being worked—played in from the side—unless they could find some cover to dodge and jerk and hide in, or a safe haven, they were pretty much consigned to death. A cruel death.

If you spend a lot of time with nature, you inevitably run into the concept, the reality of death. It comes to all living things. While now and then you hear somebody talking about how ". . . beautiful and elegant the predator-prey relationship is, how natural and proper the death of the prey is," it is usually so much misunderstood balderdash by people who have not witnessed it very many times, or worse, by people who have witnessed only highly edited versions on film.

In truth it is always cruel. It is often said that nature has no disdain, and therefore the natural death lacks the concept of anger, of revenge, of meanness, and that it is even sometimes—shudder—beautiful.

Perhaps. But only in the way the stupid, bloody slaughter of a bull in a bullfight can be called beautiful. The truth is the bull is virtually maimed and tortured, hacked and cut and stabbed until it is near death and then ceremoniously stabbed with a sword. Conversely, most animals do not kill before they eat, and the prey is often eaten slowly, miserably, and alive—in great torture and pain.

While initially as a hunter/trapper when a child, and also later, I had witnessed the concept and reality of death. As new knowledge it had now become something of less interest to me—especially after having worked on an ambulance for two years with the attendant horror and nightmares that go with that—and I no longer had that first blush of excitement or thought I had a need to know.

I decided not to see this particular story play out—rabbits in particular make a soul-searing scream as they are eaten and die—and I started to turn the mare, had already turned my own head away when I noticed that the mare had not; she had, in fact, turned slightly to face the coyotes and rabbit. She was a strange and in some ways wonderful horse, capable of an odd interest in things and now and then great compassion. I watched her one day walking along, her nose down, studying a lizard in its meanderings, and once, when riding with a friend who had brought a very old deaf and blind little female dog for the ride, I saw the mare do something I would not have believed, nor would my friend, had we not both seen it. The little dog had always led the way and now, though severely handicapped, still walked in front, still led, or tried to as we moved up an old mining road/trail in the mountains near my home. The dog became slower and slower and the horses slower behind her until, finally, she stopped and stood, staring at the ground, lost.

The mare hesitated and reached her head down, and I worried because there are some horses, many horses, who will not put up with dogs. I was concerned that the mare might bite or kick or stomp her. But no, I was wrong;

instead she took the front of her nose, that big, soft, quivering, gentle nose, put it against the little dog's rear end, and ever so gently nudge/pushed her along so she could stay ahead of us, stay as the leader. It was just the kindest, sweetest thing. . . .

And now she had stopped, was watching the story unfold below us on the dry lake. I turned to watch with her and was surprised to see there had been a change.

The jackrabbit had dodged, dug in, taken a hard right turn, which apparently surprised the coyotes enough to throw their pace off so that the rabbit maintained at least a small lead.

Coming straight at us.

The dynamic had changed completely. Where the jackrabbit had been running straight and flat on the surface of the lake with a coyote slightly to the rear on either side, the rabbit's only hope was to outrun the coyotes in a straight run—a vain hope. But now he left the lake, crossed the ancient shoreline into more broken country—easier for him to navigate, slightly harder for the coyotes, and for a moment as he dodged and zipped back and forth, he actually gained slightly, the coyotes' heavier bodies slowing them as they zigged and zagged, trying to catch him.

Somehow I did not figure us—the horse and me—into the equation. In the past I'd had prey—in my case a snowshoe hare—come in and sit by me near a fire to avoid almost certain death by a weasel; and a wonderful old fisherman named Chris Tormundsen told me of a doe, a small deer, that ran out on the ice and jumped into his boat with him on Lake Superior to avoid being captured by a pack of wolves. And again, I had a small doe—almost a fawn, barely out of spots—jump into a canoe with me as I sat fishing near the shore of a small lake in Minnesota to avoid being caught by domestic dogs. Or nearly jump into the canoe. The effect was only a little short of biblical, with barking, gurgling, screaming dogs, swearing, gurgling, screaming fisherman, and a thrashing, tearing, panicking doe in a mess of rolling canoe, mud, and water. . . .

This somehow seemed more detached, as if I were really not in the picture and only an observer.

For the moment.

Then, suddenly, everything was upon us. The rabbit zigged one last time around a scruffy boulder, ducked under an ancient century plant and stopped—dead—directly beneath the mare. Everything happened very fast, or I thought it would. The mare—Betty is her name (yet another Betty in my life)—always took a very dim view of quick surprises. I will remember forever some of what happened when a balloon that had caught under a bush jiggled loose and floated up into her nose out of nowhere. The balloon had a face painted on it, a grimacing face, a face, apparently, meant to scare the pee-wadden (I do not know what that means; it's something my grandmother always said) out of horses, and I went from sitting in the saddle to sitting in an ocotillo cactus with no horse in sight and no knowledge about how it had happened.

Heaven knew *what* would happen with a rabbit and two coyotes jammed in beneath her, and I had just about half a second to get ready for it when I realized I was mistaken. . . .

Nothing happened.

The rabbit made one last smoking effort and came to a dust-explosive shuddering stop directly beneath the mare. . . .

Who stood, absolutely still, looking first down between her front legs back at the rabbit beneath her and the two coyotes, who were standing, panting deeply, about twenty yards away. They were scruffy-looking buggers—very much like the coyotes in cartoons—and clearly not happy with events. But they were both older and wiser coyotes and knew that even if I did not somehow intervene, coming under the mare to take the rabbit would be tantamount to committing suicide.

So they held back.

A time passed. Maybe thirty seconds.

The mare took a slow, cautious step.

The rabbit hopped forward, holding his pace to match that of the mare. The mare took another step, two, three, and the rabbit matched it, following along beneath her. I turned to see the two coyotes following, about thirty feet to the rear, slightly to either side.

Oh, I thought, *good*. A parade.

How long could it last? How long would the rabbit stay sheltered under her? How long would she put up with it—and why—before she exploded and dumped me in a pile of cactus? How long before the coyotes figured out a strategy to dislodge the rabbit? If two trains started from opposite ends of the track and one train was going forty miles an hour and the other twenty miles an hour, how long would it take . . . ?

What, I thought, could I do to settle this thing? In the end I knew there was nothing and, in the end, it settled itself.

A roadrunner chased a small lizard from the left side in front of our traveling animal cavalcade. The lizard hopped, the roadrunner leaped, flapped its wings, and flew, banking directly into and past the coyotes, who instinctively took after the bird, directly away from the rabbit, who took the opportunity to disappear into a thick stand of tangled, thorny mesquite. The mare twitched twice with her whole body, lunged left, then right, and tore off after the coyotes as if she had discovered a new kind of follow-the-leader. For a quarter, then half a mile, she fairly smoked after the coyotes until they ran out into the dry river/lake bed once again. There she stopped, breathing deeply, watching the coyotes disappear in the distance.

I stood down and loosened the cinch and let her breathe all she could take in and thought once more of how often I seemed to control things from my supposed platform of being a human, and therefore a superior being. My life had for the last half hour been completely controlled by a horse, two coyotes, a roadrunner, and a jackrabbit. Not to mention the lizard. I was merely along for the ride—very precariously, as it turned out—which reminded me once again how really minor man can be when it comes to competing for space and time and food.

Or water, as I would come to see when I witnessed the outbreak of interspecies war in a highway rest stop driving through Arizona.

I had purchased an old sailboat, which I wanted to use to explore the Pacific, and I kept this boat in Ventura, California. I lived then in a shack in the southern desert mountains of New Mexico, and the drive between the boat and the shack took almost exactly thirteen hours on Interstate 10. In the three years it took me to rebuild the boat, I seemed almost to live on that highway. All the rest areas in three states became as familiar as my home.

At first it was not too crowded. Sometimes on the weekends there would be what might be called excessive traffic, but I confined my driving to the weekdays and it did not get thick until I was close to Southern California. But then air travel became more and more difficult and time-consuming due to enhanced security and driving grew much more attractive and comforting, and consequently, the highway quickly became a thronging hive of cars, trucks, vans, thousands (it seemed) of motorcycles, and huge families traveling together—especially approaching any holiday, like Easter or Christmas.

As an adjunct to this increase in traffic, the population at the highway rest areas virtually exploded. It was common to find no parking spaces available and even more common to see crowds of people—scores, hundreds of them—stopping to rest, stretch, get a drink of water (more on this later), and (it seemed) let their children run wild.

And this fact—children running amok—was perhaps the primary factor leading to the war.

All the rest areas were built along isolated stretches of the highway—sensibly, since you want them where other facilities were not available. And it must be noted that the surrounding country where they were located was stark desert and not exactly crawling with wildlife.

Still, what wilderness there was quickly came into contact—perhaps a better word would be "collision"—with the area itself and the people who were stopping there.

First, the birds.

I had spent almost my entire life misjudging birds. For some reason I thought them stupid and then found initially from parrots, mynah birds, crows, and ravens that they are indeed not only *not* ignorant and stupid but in many cases smarter than people. Still later I found that even the smallest birds—sparrows, wrens, chickadees—had wonderful innate intelligence, could work complicated math problems, and live—actually make a living and a family and *live*—in weather and conditions that would drop a human dead in his tracks.

It was in fact in the rest areas in the deserts of Arizona

and New Mexico that I first saw the smaller birds make use of this intellect. It was as a child in the Philippine Islands that I saw larger birds make use of thinking ability. In 1946 we lived in a camp outside of Manila, which came in constant contact with belligerent soldiers called "Huks." They would attack the fences at night and were driven off with machine-gun fire. This fire was often deadly accurate and resulted in casualties among the attackers—so often that it was quite usual in the mornings to see their bodies along the wire. Many of these attackers carried rations—most often rice balls. There were wild chickens almost everywhere—literally thousands of them—and they soon came to learn that machine-gun fire resulted in a chance to get at the rations or other food, and they would come running if they heard automatic weapons firing, trying to find the rice balls among the bodies of the casualties. I was walking down a gravel road one day past a machine-gun post when they fired a short burst in the air to check out some part of their weapon—machine-gun fire was very common—and I was surprised to see dozens of chickens come running out of the brushy jungle as if attacking the machine-gun position—clearly disappointed when there were no bodies to check.

Similarly, the small birds in the rest areas began to learn that the automobiles and trucks that came roaring in brought with them a wonderful smorgasbord of insects

caught and carried in their radiator grilles. Especially as spring came and the insects began their chains of reproduction; radiators became literally packed with insects, and birds flocked to the moving harvest. At first there was some confusion and open bickering; while the truck grilles were spread and open and bigger birds could get at them, many of the smaller, compact cars were limited and only small birds could get inside. Still, in the beginning the bigger birds would try the smaller cars, get trapped, and raise holy Hannah trying to get out before the tourists drove off with them trapped inside.

They seemed to learn fast, however, and soon—within

days and even hours, in some cases—small birds were hitting small cars and larger birds were hitting the trucks and larger vehicles. It seemed, however, to go almost too smoothly, and I spent more time at one of the busier rest areas and learned after lengthy study that the choreography was being controlled by some of the larger birds. These birds were scraggly-looking black birds—we used to call them "grackles." They were just a bit smaller than crows, moving in migration in large, sometimes huge, flocks. They were individually very pushy, almost cocky or snappy birds, seemingly quick to anger and push others around, much as the behavior they would use to keep someone from messing with their nest. They would rush and peck at both small and large birds who were feeding in the wrong size vehicle and, furthermore, they policed each vehicle to make certain the birds "assigned" to their radiator did a good job of cleaning out the bug carcasses.

Or so it looked. In any event, I was stunned at what I was watching; the organization, the conceptualization, the pure order of what I was seeing floored me, and then it changed again, grew. The grackles seemed to study what they had done and decided there was another ingredient, or perhaps a further dynamic that threatened to upset the order.

The people.

In the rapid movement and shuffle of birds and vehicles and radiator grilles, the tourists did not seem to recognize their positional importance in the flow of order. To wit: If they came back to their cars or trucks too soon, the birds at that particular radiator would miss out on some amount of food.

It was too clearly a waste, and the grackles set out at once to remedy the situation. If they saw somebody heading for their car before they thought it was time, they would use the "defend the nest" procedure—diving and fluttering their wings and pecking at the person's hair—to alarm them and push them back from their cars.

It was not 100 percent effective, but it started a kind of discomfort or panicked reaction, and people in general— there were about thirty people at that time in the rest area, with ten or fifteen arriving and departing—began moving in back-and-forth directions without quite knowing why they did so.

At this moment the bees entered the picture, taking over the water and finishing the job of conquering the rest area.

Obviously, it was not a planned operation—how could it be?—but the effect was the same. The water inside the bathrooms was not potable and was separate and sealed in the rooms by tight doors. This threw the only supply of drinking water on a small drinking fountain about twenty feet from the bathroom doors, and the heavy use of this fountain and perhaps lack of maintenance had caused it to leak with a steady trickle so that there was water there all the time and not just when the button was pushed.

This was on a very hot day in the middle of the Arizona desert.

Water was so valuable to all living things as to be virtually incalculable, and a colony of bees (I think killer bees, based on their aggressiveness, but I wasn't sure how to tell) discovered the steady stream of fresh, cool water about the same time as a troop of traveling schoolchildren from two vans with some kind of church group.

The children were thirsty and crowded around the fountain.

The bees were thirsty and decided to defend the same fountain.

The grackles became furious because traffic to and from the vehicles wasn't moving right, and so they lined up to begin dive-bombing just about everybody.

There was a moment, just a moment, like the hesitation in a cheap Western movie just before the gunfight starts.

Then it broke loose.

A bee, or perhaps two or three, hit a child or perhaps two or three.

Somebody screamed.

I got in my car.

And everybody ran everywhere, yelling and screaming as the bees continued their attack, and the grackles—
joined by other birds—kept trying to herd them. Some got
into the wrong vehicles—any port in a storm—some ran
for the toilets (irrespective of gender), quite a few of them
just ran (I swear I saw a trucker making close to twenty
miles an hour in rubber flip-flops heading out for the free-
way), and not a few loped off into the desert, where they
discovered cactus, assorted thorns, and heaven knows how
many different kinds of stinging bugs and reptiles.

It was, all in all, a grand example of interspecies lack of

cooperation and the further illustration that might makes right. I stayed in the rest area, in my car, for another half an hour, until everything had settled down, and saw who emerged as the victor.

The bees kept the water fountain.

CHAPTER FIVE

On the Need for a Murder of Ravens to Maintain Control of Just About Everything; and Laughing Dinosaurs

Living in nature is so strange. . . .

Memories take on life, a valid life, that is more vital, more real than the actual event. It is, in some sense, much like scurvy, an illness brought about by a lack of vitamin C, common to sailors in navies of old who could not carry enough fresh food on long sailing voyages. One of the prime symptoms of scurvy, of advanced scurvy—along with complete tooth loss and eventual madness and death— was that old wounds or ancient surgeries would open up and become fresh, with all the attendant pain and horror. A combat wound, well healed, such as a leg blown off by cannon fire, would become new, open, horrible, even after decades of healing.

And so with memories from nature. An accident—say from a moose attack or the like—perhaps because there is more time to dwell upon it, does not lessen, but in some ways grows, fills out. It would be a true nightmare except that at the same time good, sweet memories are given even more strength, more reality.

I can remember with incredible detail my grandmother baking me an apple pie and sitting with me with two glasses of chilled whole milk on a day when I stepped on a rusty sixteen-penny nail sticking through an old board at the back of the barn. The nail is almost gone from my mind, but the pie, with sugar and cinnamon sprinkled on top, hot from the oven, the cold milk, my grandmother's soothing, melodic voice telling me in Norwegian that I—that it—would all be fine has filled the memory with such pleasantness, such joy that there is no room for the misery. . . .

And the same rule seems to apply to all "natural" memories. I have written much about the woods, being in the woods, being in nature, as it was for me a very real kind of sanctuary—a safe place. A truly safe place. A beautiful place. And yet . . .

And yet.

I have been attacked by moose, charged by bear, run down by feral dog packs, struck by rattlesnakes, bump-attacked by sharks . . . even put on top of my car by an angry weasel not much bigger than my thumb. (I thought, later, that he might have rabies, but at the time I merely jumped in fear.)

It's just that those things don't seem to have the weight, the measureless beauty of countless sunsets and dawns, the simple grace and clear glory of nature. And besides, often it is the bad things that turn out to be the best. I fell off a dogsled down a frozen waterfall and landed on sharp ice on a kneecap. It was so agonizing, I thought, seriously, that my heart would stop. But I found that my whole dog team loved and worried about me so much, they curved downstream and worked back up to me to surround me as I lay clutching my lacerated knee, whimpering and pushing their warm bodies against me. I remember the love, the dog love, much more than the shattered knee. . . .

And it was one of the ugliest of things that brought ravens into my life and made them my medicine bird.

It is perhaps true that nobody should trap wild animals. I have done so—as a young boy, and then, when destroyed financially and forced to go back to the woods, as an adult for a couple of years. I wasted nothing, fed the meat to my dogs or ate it myself, tanned or sold the pelts, did everything legal by state and federal law, worked within the ecology to help keep a correct balance in nature, and yet . . .

And yet. If there is such a thing as hell, I think I will be consigned there for trapping. The animals had no choice in it, and even if the state tells you beaver must be thinned because they are ruining highways, or coyotes must be taken as they are wiping out sheep ranchers, the animals still do not understand or know these things—how they, how we work. They simply know they are alive one day and dead the next—for no apparent reason. And so I think that even if there is a reason, it may be wrong.

Still, there is something worse than just trapping, and that is to trap without sense or judgment or responsibility, and shame that it may be, such things happen.

It is how I met ravens.

I was trapping in northern Minnesota and somebody had crossed my line and set steel leg-hold traps (I used only snares) with bait—which was illegal—and hung the meat bait on a wire directly up and over the trap, forcing an animal to stand in the trap to reach the bait (also illegal); plus they were fairly large traps. I was running my team up a small frozen creek when I came around a corner and saw a raven caught in a number-four steel trap. Drawn by the bait, he had stepped full on the trip pad, and the jaws had caught his foot before he could react and escape.

By one toe.

Just the end of it, barely.

And he was absolutely furious. I mean, there is anger and frustrated anger or anger mixed with fear or anger mixed with only slightly diluted rabid madness, and he was all of them, way past all of them. He was huge, like a big, black, squawking, enraged and murderous turkey, and if he'd had a gun, or a knife, or access to a nuclear device, I would have been gone instantly. A flock of ravens is called a "murder," and now I could see why.

The dog team was barreling up the creek and was drawn in by his commotion, and I barely got the sled stopped and tied off to a tree before they got to him. They would have torn him to pieces, but he didn't care. He jerked at the chain and tried to get loose, not to get away from the dogs but to get at them—I mean, it was complete insanity.

"A minute," I said. "Let me get you out of there. It will just take a minute. . . ." I had seen crows and one other raven in traps but never with this kind of rage. And the *noise* he was making! It was beyond even rudimentary, infantry, truck-driver jailhouse swearing—I know he condemned me to eight or nine slow deaths.

I stood on the two trap springs and released the jaws, and he pecked at my legs, slamming his beak against my thick winter pants. When he got loose, he flew up at my face before I could cover it, tried for my eyes and then—I swear—whipped over backward and took a shot at Cookie, my lead dog. Surprised, rather than rip him up, she ducked, and he swerved back at me, barely missed my eyes again, then wheeled up into a tree.

Where he sat.

Swearing.

I gathered gear, left the trap triggered and hanging from a branch, and made my way back up the creek. He followed, swearing each time I stopped with a language that clearly indicated he had many different words available for enraged cursing.

Finally, at the end of the day, when I camped, he moved off and I did not see him again. Or I should say I did not see *him* again, but many times—past counting—in places where you would least expect it, often under duress or when things were either going bad or about to go bad, there would be a raven. Often silent, sometimes swearing, always pointedly looking at me, neck feathers ruffled, wings half out, beak extended.

An example: I had sailed down from Alaska to California in my small boat, and for a good night's sleep I had anchored in a cove south of Monterey called San Simeon, near where they built the Hearst Castle just north of Morro Bay. I slept a solid night into midmorning and was having a cup of tea in the new sun when I looked up, and just over the boat, straight up, glided an osprey looking for a fish. He was beautiful and wonderfully graceful.

Just as I wondered if I could get a picture of him up there in the sun, a raven came rushing in from the side and attacked him.

This is not rare. All birds hate raptors and crows, and ravens attack them constantly. But this osprey was clever, and though the raven grabbed a wing feather, it twisted loose before the raven could peck his eyes (the common attack—to cause blindness) and the osprey flew off, gaining altitude, and the raven dropped the feather and flew away as well.

I watched as the feather drifted and circled and circled and drifted down until it landed on my boat not a foot from where I was standing.

It was beautiful, clearly lined and barred, and I picked it up, felt that it was an omen of grace and flight and tied it to the mast down inside the boat.

A beautiful, innocent encounter, you might say.

And so I thought.

But remember the raven. . . .

Fully eight months later, I was in a boatyard farther south in California, getting my bottom paint renewed, and there was a state or county peace officer in the same boatyard. We started talking, and I invited him aboard my boat for a cup of tea. We talked longer there about the sad state of the oceans, when suddenly he stopped and looked at the feather on the mast.

"Where did you get that?" he asked.

I told him, in detail, because I liked the story and there was such beauty in it.

"That's a raptor feather. . . ."

"I know. Isn't it beautiful?"

"It's five years in a federal prison and a twenty-five-thousand-dollar fine. . . ."

Wow, I thought, *some feather.*

He confiscated it and did not arrest me—for which I am eternally grateful—and I sailed on into my life. Perhaps a week later, while thinking of the incident again, I remembered something that had slipped my mind.

The raven.

He had pulled the wing feather out of the osprey. And he had dropped it. And it landed on me. And I know, I know what seems obvious—that it was probably an accident.

But I was the one who could have done five years in a federal prison, not the raven. And if it looks like a duck and quacks like a duck and walks like a duck, it's me; I'm the duck, not the raven. I would be the duck doing time.

Proof of this possibly evil, or at least cantankerous connection, would come just a year later.

Everything, it seems, moves in a circle. Life keeps whipping around and around, and on my last go-around, the Iditarod raised its furry canine head. I knew, or thought I knew, that I hadn't finished with it yet. I was wrong, of course, and old, and brittle, and not a little stupid, but I would have to break legs and arms and wrists and have another tooth kicked out before I began to believe in my own ability to commit errors. So I borrowed all the money I could, bought forty-six dogs and a couple of sleds and an old house back in the woods in Alaska a hundred plus miles north of Anchorage, and settled in to train for and run the Iditarod for the third time. (I finished it in 1983 and almost finished it again in 1985.) My body was then sixty-five years old, but my brain—in a scientific achievement of incredible adeptness—had stopped at the age of thirty-eight or so, and with wonderful abilities of delusion convinced me that this would all work. What's even more amazing is that I am now sitting here, writing this at the age of seventy-three, and what passes for my brain is *still* working at me to go back and try it again. Hmmm.

It is like a symphony musician who stops playing a piece on a hanging note and he cannot rest until he finishes the note.

So I went back again, put the dogs on the glacier in Juneau, and moved farther north to build a kennel, which was when I ran into the grizzly bear, then went to the pound and got Corky the poodle to watch my back. He is sitting behind me now. Although he is very old, losing vision and hearing, he's still watching, still in his mind only thirty-eight or so (in people years), fully capable of taking out a grizzly. In his mind.

So we worked all that summer, put in a kennel, bought six old freezers for dog food, brought the dogs back from the glacier in late fall, began feeding meat, and then the company came.

Full circle, remember?

The ravens.

Leo, my friend and dog handler—who is taking care of the dogs now as I work in the Lower 48 on some business problems—was originally from the city, and it was a jolt to move into the bush. As it would be for anybody.

When the ravens first came, it was one or two birds. They sat in the trees around the kennel simply observing—taking notes—which they shared with one another using bill clicking as a form of semi-telegraphic communication. We had acquired four all-terrain vehicles—two small ones and two slightly larger—which we pulled with teams on woodland trails before there was snow for sleds. It worked the dogs harder than the light aluminum and plastic sleds and so we started them right off on a strong meat diet: beef hearts, which we purchased in sixty-pound boxes and cut into small one-inch chunks when we fed.

And the two scout ravens (as we found them to be) saw this meat. While they are largely omnivorous, anything as rich and full of energy as straight heart meat could not be ignored, and after a week the two birds left.

And returned the next day with twenty-eight friends.

We suddenly had thirty ravens, and they set out immediately to rearrange our situation so it would be *their* situation, much as the birds and bees had done in the highway rest areas.

First they had to train the dogs. Forty or so sled dogs, stone carnivores, each in his own insulated house with a twelve-foot chain, capable of lightning-fast reflexes and lunges, require a lot of training, and the ravens set out immediately with a distinct method.

Three ravens would hang around a specific dog, teasing him by getting closer and then jumping back, working at him most of a day, tease and jump, tease and jump, until, finally, the dog would get sick of it and began to ignore the ravens.

Then would come feeding time—twice a day. Each dog

got a large bowl with beef heart and commercial dog food mixed with warm water. They loved it, hit it like wolves, and the ravens would have to move off, start over and retrain them. Initially it was slow work, but the dogs had been preconditioned by the daily training, and two ravens would come at the bowl from the side, drawing the dog away while a third hit the food and dragged off a piece of meat. They would do this again and again until at last, at long last (and the ravens were wonderfully patient), the dog would sit back, relax, and simply let the ravens pick through and take out the best parts before letting the dog have his go. We, the humans, were being trained as well in that we added special bits of meat for the ravens so the dogs wouldn't go hungry. I once saw a kennel in Canada where they fed more than a hundred puppies twice a day in large, rubberized circular dish troughs, and when it came time to feed, the puppies—trained to a T—ran screaming in circles around the dishes until the ravens (perhaps fifty of them) had carefully, and slowly, picked through the food for themselves before letting the pups in.

Having trained us and our dogs—it took about two weeks to complete—the ravens set about altering, or trying to alter, the rest of our regimen to fit their needs.

They hated the four small all-terrain vehicles. Either due to the noise of the motors or (and I think this was the real reason) because we were constantly harnessing the dogs and hooking them to the four-wheelers and taking off on long runs, where we would stop and feed them in the bush. That took the dogs away from the ravens (their true masters) during feeding time.

So I went out one morning and the ignition keys for two of the four-wheelers were gone. The other two sets were still in the ignitions, but the first two were missing.

Just like that. I saw Leo on the other side of the kennel, and knowing that he was from a semi-urban environment in the Lower 48 and perhaps was worried about theft (all but impossible in the bush where we lived), I called:

"We don't have to pull the keys on the four-wheelers."

"I haven't touched them. . . ."

And even as I watched, a large raven landed on one of the four-wheelers, reached up, and deftly pulled the ignition key out of its slot and threw it on the ground, hopped to the remaining machine, pulled the key, threw it down, and then flew away.

They knew. They had watched us with the four-wheelers and knew that we used the key to start them, to run them, and by pulling the key would keep us from running dogs with them, from taking away the food on long runs.

I wondered then, for the first real time, how much of our intelligence, or supposed intellect, which made us feel superior and full of manifest destiny—how much of that was and is purely self-delusional—and I knew. Knew so surely that it brought a cold feeling to the back of my neck—a cold, self-delusional little breeze back there.

All?

Is it all just us deceiving ourselves?

So we found the keys on the ground and wire-tied them back into the machines so the ravens couldn't pull them out, thwarting them just this once, just now an insult to them, so that they had one more thing to say, one more thought.

The next morning, just daylight, I went out into the kennel to sip tea and be with the dogs before feeding time.

The morning sounds were so soft, so gentle and relaxing.

And there, on the ground in front of one of the best lead dogs, lay something new—half an orange, cut and juiced.

Just sitting there.

And when I looked around the kennel, I could see more of them, dozens, scores of them, scattered in front of the dogs. Leo came out of his cabin then, and I asked him if he'd been eating oranges and juicing them and throwing the peels into the kennel; I knew better, but I asked anyway.

"I don't eat oranges. . . ."

Of course he didn't. I knew better. And as I stood there, overhead came a wave of eight or ten ravens, flying in from the east, where, a mile away, a family with children lived, and I knew I would find that they ate oranges that had been juiced and they threw their peelings on a compost pile and the ravens were picking them up and flying a mile back and bombing the kennel with them.

An answer.

An answer to the wired-in ignition keys. Garbage on our heads. Humor?

A prank?

And I picked up an orange peel and knew that no matter what we did, the ravens would be there, would always be there, at least one step ahead of us.

And that brought perhaps a new bit of knowledge to

come from the ravens: They, and all birds, are said to have descended from the dinosaurs. Extrapolating backward and knowing that the dinosaurs had literally millions of years to evolve, grow, and perfect what they were, isn't it probable that if a raven could make jokes, could make pranks, could drop orange peelings on my head:

Couldn't dinosaurs laugh?

INTERROGATUM: THREE THINGS TO LEARN

1. When a lawn mower goes over a lawn with tall dandelions in it and cuts them down, the stalks never grow back up above the height of the mower blade. How do they know it and how do they tell the plant to stay below this certain height, as if measured?

2. If an earthworm is placed in a glass tube with two forks and in one of the forks a wire with a tiny bit of electricity is placed so that if the worm goes up that fork and hits the electricity it will feel mild discomfort, then that worm will always go up the other fork. While they have small ganglia, earthworms have no real brain and probably no forms of communication other than chemical slime and so probably no real memory. If placed with another worm who has never been in the glass tube and then separated and the new worm is let go in a glass with two forks, the new worm will always take the "safe" fork, as if he'd been told. How can this be?

3. It is said that the weight of all the ants on the planet far exceeds the weight of all humans on the planet and that in organization and numbers ants far exceed humans. They will, for instance, kidnap eggs from

other ant mounds, hatch them out, raise them, and use them as slaves—a level it was thought only humans had sunk to. Does all this not make ants the largest and most successful species on the planet?

GARY PAULSEN is one of the most honored writers of contemporary literature for young readers, and the author of three Newbery Honor titles: *Dogsong*, *Hatchet*, and *The Winter Room*. He has written more than two hundred books for adults and young readers. He divides his time between New Mexico, Alaska, and on the Pacific.